A Short Introduction to Critical Old Testament Methodologies

A Short Introduction to Critical Old Testament Methodologies

ROBERT KARL GNUSE

CASCADE *Books* • Eugene, Oregon

A SHORT INTRODUCTION TO CRITICAL OLD TESTAMENT
METHODOLOGIES

Cascade Books
An Imprint of Wipf and Stock Publishers
199 W. 8th Ave., Suite 3
Eugene, OR 97401

www.wipfandstock.com

PAPERBACK ISBN: 979-8-3852-3991-7
HARDCOVER ISBN: 979-8-3852-3992-4
EBOOK ISBN: 979-8-3852-3993-1

Cataloguing-in-Publication data:

Names: Robert Karl Gnuse, 1947–, author.
Title: A short introduction to critical Old Testament methodologies / Robert
   Karl Gnuse.
Description: Eugene, OR: Cascade Books, 2025. | Includes bibliographical refer-
   ences.
Identifiers: ISBN 979-8-3852-3991-7 (paperback). | ISBN 979-8-3852-3992-4
   (hardcover). | ISBN 979-8-3852-3993-1 (ebook).
Subjects: LCSH: Bible.—Old Testament—Criticism, interpretation, etc.—
   Methodology. | Bible.—Old Testament—Hermeneutics.
Classification: BS476.G59 2025 (print). | BS476 (ebook).

VERSION NUMBER 10/20/25

CONTENTS

PREFACE

The Method of Biblical Study

PROFESSIONAL BIBLICAL SCHOLARS AND theologians engage in a reading of the text designed to perceive more precisely what the text is saying, to intuit what was in the mind of the author, and to understand more clearly what was said to the original audience. When contemporary readers understand what the original message was, it becomes easier to draw good parallel implications for today's believers. Informed intuitions about what the text originally meant provide substance for biblical theologians to weave their craft and offer creative thoughts for preachers to expound upon in their sermons. Such informed intuitions about the messages of biblical texts also prevent egregious misrepresentations, which so often lead to the oppression of people, especially of women, minorities, and gay people, and to an apathy about helping the poor. A classmate of mine who teaches German and political science at Texas A & M likes to say that he is a socialist, not because of his study of political science but because he read the New Testament critically in Greek. The greatest misinterpretations of the Bible result from misunderstanding what the original message meant, thus misrepresenting what it could mean for us.

For two thousand years, theologians have sought to understand the text correctly, but the task is not easy, as the multiplicity of interpretations by good Christians demonstrates, and the dialectical theological positions of Christian denominations indicate. Even within any one denomination, there will be differences of interpretation over at least some minor issues. This will never cease as long as we remain finite human beings. However, the Judeo-Christian tradition has been blessed in the past two centuries by the development of archaeological skills, knowledge of ancient history, and new ways of reading the biblical text in the light of its social and historical context. We know more about biblical language and culture than we ever have before. Biblical exegetes of all traditions have come to better understand the biblical message. As a result, we have learned to appreciate what unites all believers and that it outweighs whatever differences divide them. We have learned to appreciate that the diverse theological views of others as well as our own are rooted in the biblical text and that the various differences which divide Christian denominational articulations, in particular, are not as great as we once were accustomed to think.

The theologian or exegete who reads the Bible in a knowledgeable fashion does so by reading it with "critical" methods. By "critical" we do not mean a spirit of disbelief or disrespect, but with the intent of penetrating to the original meaning and the best message for today. The reader may try to be "critical" of whatever he or she was previously taught about a passage in order to read the text fresh and let it speak on its own. If you sometimes suspend your assumptions about what a passage says, you will not surrender your religious faith, but you might discover a new insight or perspective you never considered previously. Critical methods of reading attempt to unlock those deeper insights. When I was in seminary, Professor Fred Danker, the Pauline specialist, told us to read Paul and forget everything we knew about him, because otherwise we could not read him in a fresh way and discover new insights from his message. We would read into him our denominational (Lutheran) teachings and thus miss what he was saying for his age, and critical methodologies would aid us in the discovery of Paul and his message.

A series of reading methods have evolved in the past century which help exegetes greatly. Taken together, these methods are called the "historical-critical" approach, which means they seek to find the meaning of a text in its original historical context by objectively reading the text. Sometimes manuals distinguish between "higher" and "lower" critical methods. "Lower criticism" refers to textual criticism, an effort to isolate the best Hebrew or Greek reading of a passage. "Higher criticism" refers to the more subjective analyses (source, form, traditio-historical) that hypothesize the shape and development of a text and sometimes produce more challenging insights. In reality, however, text criticism may be equally challenging and raise even more problems. Thus, many scholars prefer not to use this distinction but simply speak of the "historical-critical method" in general.

Throughout the twentieth century and to the present day the Roman Catholic Church has affirmed the use of this method when it is used by people of the faith to articulate teachings which edify Christians and strengthen the Christian mission and the proclamation of the gospel. For example, the magisterium of the Roman Catholic Church issued two encyclicals (*Providentissimus Deus*, 1893, and *Divino Afflante Spiritu*, 1943) and a significant conciliar document of Vatican II (*Dei Verbum*, 1965) discussing the church's use of this critical method. The latest two documents, in particular, have greatly encouraged the use of the critical method by Roman Catholic scholars over the past two generations. The publication of those two documents ushered in, one might be tempted to say, a "golden age" of biblical scholarship among Roman Catholic scholars, especially in America.

In this little volume, I will give a brief characterization of the important aspects of that method, which now is taught routinely to seminarians and those who teach religion or Bible on the secondary and college level. When I was in seminary in the 1970s, I was impressed by a volume written by Klaus Koch: *The Growth of the Biblical Tradition: The Form-Critical Method* (which I'll reference as Koch); it explained the critical method and then provided biblical texts as examples of that method. I decided to do that on a more comprehensive scale for each of the methods, for I believe that it is best to provide an example of a text and not just to describe the critical method abstractly.

Preface

Unlike most writers of introductions to critical methodologies, I will not spend extensive space and effort describing the history of the method. I will briefly mention some of the great scholars who inspired the method, but I will not go into detail describing the content of their seminal writings in this regard. The student is more interested in the nature of the methodology, I believe, rather than in the history. Furthermore, those great scholars often wrote in the early twentieth century (or the late nineteenth), and we are now in the twenty-first century. We need to move on and no longer be fixated on talking about those great authors as much as introductions have been in the past.

The first chapters describe the traditional historical-critical methods: *text criticism, source criticism, form criticism,* and *traditio-historical criticism.* The latter chapters endeavor to explain the new methodologies that have arisen in the past sixty years. I have classified them into two categories: *new literary criticism* and *intellectual criticism.* This classification is my own, based on my perceptions, and not all may agree with it. But the purpose of this little volume is to give a basic explanation of the criticisms biblical scholars use, and this will be accomplished regardless of my classifications. Special attention is also given to *canonical criticism* and *social-scientific criticism,* which I believe are not really methodological criticisms used to probe the biblical texts; rather they are scholarly and theological approaches that can be combined with the other methodologies. But many scholars refer to them as critical approaches, so they merit attention in a volume such as this.

The text of this volume is designed to be an introduction, but it does assume familiarity with the biblical text. It is best used by religious studies majors in colleges or for introductory exegetical courses on the seminary level. Its shortness enables it to be used with other textbooks in a course on the Bible and its interpretation.

I would like to thank New Orleans Baptist Theological Seminary for the use of their facilities over many years in the generation of this volume. I thank Wipf and Stock Publishers for the permission to reprint portions of pp. 200–216 of my book *Misunderstood*

Stories: Theological Commentary on Genesis 1–11 (Eugene, OR: Cascade Books, 2014) in chapter 3 of this volume.

I thank the editors of the *International Journal of Research in Humanities and Social Studies* for permission to reprint the last half of my article "Deuteronomic Redaction and the Evolution of the Decalogues in Exodus 20 and Deuteronomy 5"—*International Journal of Research in Humanities and Social Studies* 11.2 (2024) 19–29—in chapter 5 of this volume. I thank Abingdon Press for permission to reprint the last two pages of my article "Tradition History"—from *Dictionary of Biblical Interpretation*, 2 vols., edited by John H. Hayes (Nashville: Abingdon, 1999), vol. 2:583–88—in chapter 5 of this volume.

I dedicate this book to Riley, Brady, and Ollie, grandchildren who might read it someday.

1

TEXT CRITICISM

Text Criticism

THIS METHOD IS CONCERNED with establishing the best or most original form of the Hebrew or Greek text. Text critics compare the oldest extant manuscripts to determine the most accurate reading for modern translations of the Bible. The critical editions that they produce, of the Hebrew Old Testament, the translated Greek version of the Old Testament, called the Septuagint, and the New Testament, all contain footnotes of the variant readings for various biblical passages. Thus, any translator may choose his or her own readings, if the translator feels justified in departing from the reading provided in the main body of the text. (This is why good Bible translations are created by committees, so that the perspectives of one translator do not create an idiosyncratic result.) Alternative readings for critical comparison are provided for the Hebrew text not only by manuscripts in Hebrew but also by translations, called the versions, which include the various Septuagintal traditions (including the revisions of Aquila, Symmachus, and Theodotion from the second century CE), the Dead Sea Scrolls (from 200 BCE to 135 CE), the Aramaic Targums (which are called paraphrases), the Syriac Peshitta, the Latin Vulgate, and even translations in Coptic and Armenian.

Critical editions of the Bible in Hebrew and Greek display in the main body of the text those readings judged by text critics to be most original, and variant readings are placed in footnotes at the bottom of the page with an abbreviation system to help the translator/reader identify the manuscript source. Critics use the following rules to determine what they believe the original reading might have been:

1. The older manuscript is often more reliable; thus we respect the Old Greek or Septuagint and the Dead Sea Scrolls.

2. The manuscript that generally has fewer overall mistakes is more reliable in individual instances, for it tells us that we can trust the copyist who replicated that manuscript.

3. The majority of manuscripts on a particular reading are to be heeded, if they agree against the Hebrew Masoretic Text.

4. Shorter readings in a particular text are preferred, since longer readings in a manuscript may be expansions by later copyists.

5. More difficult readings are preferred since copyists often try to clarify confusing or difficult passages (unless one can explain how a difficult reading arose due to poor copying).

6. Determining what reasonably could have given rise to the mistake in the text can justify a change or emendation.

7. A number of typical mistakes are introduced by copyists, and textual critics are alert to spot those in creating an original text:

   (a) Sometimes scribes missed lines when their eyes jumped downward to a phrase that was repeated (*homoeoteleuton* or *homoeoarchton*).

   (b) Sometimes their eyes jumped upward to a similar expression, and they repeated some lines (*dittography*).

   (c) Sometimes the scribe wrote once what was supposed to be written twice (*haplography*).

(d) Occasionally, words were misspelled because letters looked like each other. This is most common with the Hebrew letters *daleth* and *resh*.

(e) Or sometimes a letter simply was written incorrectly, and what should have been one Hebrew word became a different word or something nonsensical.

(f) Sometimes two Hebrew words had the letters divided incorrectly between them. This was especially possible in Hebrew because only consonants were written down in the manuscripts until 800 CE, and all the words were placed together without spaces between them.

(g) Sometimes a letter was simply left out, creating a different word from what was likely intended.

So often the result of these mistakes is a rather bizarre message or one that is awkward at least. Thus, the text critic in all these instances feels that when the Septuagint offers a better translation and the Hebrew can be explained by one of the aforementioned mistakes, the Hebrew should be emended. Yet the haunting possibility remains that the Hebrew, however odd it may be, could be the correct reading. But if there is one overarching rule with all these instances, when you are convinced that you should emend the Hebrew text, it is to use common sense. So, although the shorter reading or the more difficult reading is to be preferred generally, if it produces a nonsense translation that cannot be made into a sensible translation, then emendation is a good option.

Essentially, text-critical scholars use many rules to construct a faithful text for use by exegetes, theologians, translators, preachers, seminarians, or anyone who can read the Bible in the original languages.

Translations and Text Traditions

We must always remember that when we speak of translations or textual traditions, we are speaking of a collection of scrolls, not actual books. Christians did not have books, or *codices* (singular: *codex*), until after 300 CE. The earliest books for Christians, were made of vellum, or sheepskin pages. Our two oldest codices from the fourth century CE are Codex Vaticanus and Codex Sinaiticus, both in Greek. The ancients who collected individual books of the Old and New Testaments in those two codices had to decide what to include and what to exclude. However, when we look at those two collections, we discover that they disagree on which books they include, both with Old and New Testament works. Christians did not officially decide which books to include in the New Testament canon until the Council of Ephesus in 431 CE. They never decided on the Old Testament writings, which is why there are at least five different versions of the Old Testament collections even today among Christians. (Coptic Christians have the most in their canon.) Jews, of course, chose only works written in Hebrew, and their early decision may have arisen among the rabbis teaching at the yeshiva in Jabneh between 96 and 132 CE and was likely accepted by most Jews after 200 CE and the appearance of the Mishnah. Throughout those early years, if you approached a priests in various Christian churches and asked to see their sacred texts, they would come out with an armload of scrolls, and that armload would be different among the Christian communities scattered all over the world.

Several factors complicate text criticism for scholars of the Old Testament or Hebrew Bible. Our oldest complete Hebrew Bible comes from the eleventh century CE (Codex Leningradensis), and fragments come to us from the ninth century CE (Cairo Codex of the Pentateuch, Cairo Codex of the Prophets, Aleppo Codex, Babylonian Codex of the Prophets), all of which are extremely distant in time from the formation of the canon. In some instances, the Dead Sea Scrolls offer us partial texts from the era 150 BCE to 50 CE. Though there really is little difference between these documents, there are some noticeable variations in particular books of the Bible. This indicates that our complete Hebrew manuscripts could be surpassed in quality by these older Hebrew texts.

The Septuagint is a Greek translation of the Old Testament that was created piecemeal between 270 BCE and 100 BCE, with some books translated perhaps as late as 100 CE. Jewish tradition in the Letter of Aristeas (120 BCE) implies that the Septuagint was translated in Egypt around 270 BCE, but in reality, a large portion of the Septuagint (abbreviated as LXX in reference to the supposed seventy Jewish translators who created it) appears to come from various translators in different eras over three hundred years. Only the Pentateuch was translated supposedly in 270 BCE. When compared to the Hebrew Bible or Masoretic Text, the Septuagint does have variant readings and, sometimes, additional stories. The Septuagint is called the Old Greek translation to differentiate it from three second-century Greek revisions of the Septuagint by Aquila, Symmachus, and Theodotion. Aquila was a Jew who was uncomfortable with the Christian use of the Old Greek text(s). Symmachus was a Samaritan. There are also several versions of the Old Greek or Septuagint, most notably the Lucianic. Text critics take their revisions into account to establish the possible original Hebrew text, and this renders the whole process of text criticism very complex. (Remember when we say Septuagint, we mean a collection of scrolls, not a book—that is, not a codex—so the Septuagint as a collection of scrolls could include different biblical books for different groups of people.) When books or codices finally became common in the fourth century CE, the two oldest Greek Bibles, Codex Sinaiticus and Codex Vaticanus, both disagreed on which books, in both the Old and the New Testaments, to include.

There are classic examples of how Greek translations challenge our version of the Hebrew Masoretic Text. The book of Jeremiah is one-eighth shorter in the Septuagint than in the Masoretic Text, because the Septuagint probably had an earlier Hebrew edition of the book of Jeremiah to translate. Thus, some scholars believe the Septuagint can be used to correct the Hebrew text because it was based on Hebrew manuscripts much older than we have. But the Septuagint still is a translation, and because many different people over the years contributed to this rather uneven translation, the quality of the variant readings is irregular, so text critics must decide on each variant on its own merit. (In college I took a course in the Septuagint, and I was amazed how the Greek in the various books is so very different, sometimes very simple, as with Tobit, and at other times intensely difficult, as with Maccabees.) For years most scholars were reluctant to use variant Septuagintal readings to correct the Masoretic Text, but with the discovery of the Dead Sea Scrolls, it was noted that often an individual Dead Sea Scroll will agree with the Septuagint against a specific reading in the Masoretic Text. Thus, the prestige of the Septuagint increased, but there was a reason; there were different versions or recensions of the Hebrew texts that evolved into the Masoretic Text.

Since the discovery of the Dead Sea Scrolls over seventy years ago, scholars have begun to sense that there was no one, original written Hebrew text that was authoritative for all Jews. Rather, there were three Hebrew textual traditions: (1) Babylonian, which evolved into our present Masoretic Text of the Hebrew Bible; (2) Egyptian, which was the basis for the Old Greek Septuagint translation; and (3) Palestinian, which may have been behind the Samaritan Pentateuch and some Aramaic commentaries used among the Jews, and which came to be known as the Targums. This theory would explain why the Septuagint differs from the Hebrew Bible at times and refutes the idea that the differences are due simply to copyists' errors. Often the Dead Sea Scrolls agree with the Septuagint against the Masoretic Text, when previously we favored the Masoretic Text. Sometimes the Septuagint might agree with the Masoretic Text against the Dead Sea Scrolls. (The actual relationships of various scrolls of these three traditions or recensions is very complex.) This is why Ezra brought a copy of the Torah or Pentateuch from Babylon in the fifth century BCE and imposed it as the standard version (presumably against other Hebrew traditions from Egypt and Palestine). These three traditions arose during and after the sixth century BCE Babylonian exile, as much of the literature—especially the Pentateuch, Deuteronomistic History, and Prophets—began as oral cycles and became written texts and text collections among exiles scattered into these various regions. If this theory is correct, it means the text critics' quest for the original text is futile, and the comparative use of the Septuagint and the Hebrew Bible becomes a more complex task. The Dead Sea Scrolls attest to the presence of all three recensions at Qumran, when you might assume the Scrolls should reflect the Palestinian recension. In the opinion of some text critics, that the Dead Sea Scrolls do not primarily reflect the Palestinian recension indicates that the three-recension theory itself is simplistic; there is a "multiplicity" of recensions, more than three. This makes the challenge even greater for text critics. But text critics love this kind of challenge. At any rate, text criticism is a superb discipline, which helps produce our contemporary and much-improved translations of the Bible.

For further reading in more detailed fashion, two excellent introductory works have been written by Ralph Klein (Klein 1974) and Kyle McCarter (McCarter 1986). Two very thorough texts were crafted by Emanuel Tov (Tov 1997, 2022).

Biblical Examples of Text Criticism

In the vast majority of instances text criticism will correct a single word or the defective spelling. But there are instances where the text critic may have discerned that something has been added to the Hebrew text, or it may discern that a copyist has accidently lost something from the Hebrew text. More significantly it has been established that little phrases were added to the book of Jeremiah in large number after the appearance of an Old Greek translation from a Hebrew text of Jeremiah.

Here is an example of where the Septuagint has a superior reading to the Masoretic Text because 1 Chr 3:18 supports the Septuagint's reading for the most part:

> 2 Sam 6:5 (MT): And David and all the house of Israel were playing before Yahweh *with all the juniper trees.*

> 2 Sam 6:5 (LXX): And David and the Sons of Israel were playing before the Lord *with harmonized instruments, with power, and with songs.*

1 Chr 3:18: And David and all Israel were playing before God *with all strength and with songs.*

The correlation is not perfect, of course, but it is clear enough that the Masoretic Hebrew should read "songs" and not "juniper trees." The change from "songs" to "juniper trees" occurred in the original Hebrew due to a slight misplacement of consonants in the noun for "songs" (Klein 48).

Sometimes it is a little more complex. In the next example, 1 Chr 18:31 most likely supports a reading in the Lucianic version of the Septuagint against both the Masoretic Text and the Old Greek Septuagint (Klein 50).

1 Kgs 22:32 (MT): And they turned against him to fight and Jehoshaphat cried out

1 Kgs 22:32 (LXX): And they surrounded him to fight and Jehoshaphat cried out

1 Kgs 22:32 (Lucianic): And they surrounded him to fight and Jehoshaphat cried out, *and the Lord saved him,*

1 Chr 18:31: And they surrounded him to fight and Jehoshaphat cried out, *and Yahweh saved him.*

Another example demonstrates how a Dead Sea Scroll (4QSamb) sides with the Septuagint against the Masoretic Text (Klein 22).

1 Sam 21:6 (MT): The vessels of the young men have been consecrated.

1 Sam 21:6 (LXX): All the young men have been consecrated.

1 Sam 21:6 (4Q Samb): All the young men have been consecrated.

As can be seen, this is a subtle art, but after working with a number of examples, the text critic will develop a good feeling about making textual decisions.

Examples wherein a copyist's eyes jumped from one line to another because the words were similar is common. This will result in words being repeated (*dittography*) or left out (*haplography*). Isa 17:12–13 appears to be an example of dittography (McCarter 32):

> Isa 17:12–13 (MT): (12) and the roar of the peoples—like the roar of mighty waters they roar (13) *of peoples—like the roar of many waters they roar.*

Or another similar example occurs in 2 Kgs 7:13 (McCarter 30):

> 2 Kgs 7:13 (MT): One of his servants answered and said, "Let five of the remaining horses be taken, for those who remain here will be like the whole multitude of Israel *for those who remain here will be like the whole multitude of Israel* who have perished. So let's send them and see."

These are simple but typical examples of text-critical issues. The text critic engages in a challenging task, for it not only demands the clear discernment of when there is a problem; the text critic must have tools in abundance, particularly lexicons of Hebrew, Aramaic, Greek, Syriac, Arabic, Coptic, and even Armenian, so as to consult the diverse textual traditions that will provide commentary on the reading of the Masoretic Text. Furthermore, the text critic must be alert to the different traditions in the Greek translations (Old Greek, Lucianic, Aquila, Symmachus, and Theodotian). The task is compounded by an awareness that there might be three textual traditions of the Masoretic Text (Babylonian: the Masoretic Text; Palestinian: the Targums and the Samaritan Pentateuch; and Egyptian: the Septuagint). The serious text critic is one who writes commentaries. This task is not for the faint of heart, but students of biblical criticism must be aware of this important endeavor.

2

SOURCE CRITICISM

ALTHOUGH IN THE PAST the term literary criticism was synony-
mous with what I'm calling source criticism in this book, today the
term literary criticism denotes rhetorical, aesthetic, and structural
methods of interpretation. It seeks to discover the original text or
source that lies behind our present text. With prophetic oracles
that would mean discerning what was the original oracle or set of
oracles that came from the oral proclamation of a specific prophet.
With Pentateuchal laws and narratives, it means discerning the
separate "sources" that were woven together to create our present
text. Biblical accounts are separated by scholars from their present
written context and are compared to other biblical accounts with
which they appear to have had a common origin. Sometimes narrative reads more smoothly when these individual stories with a
common origin are connected (or reconnected) with each other.
Until the 1930s we spoke of these various sources behind our text
as though they were written literature; hence, they were called
documents, and the theory informing source criticism was called
the Documentary Hypothesis. Since then, we have perceived that
the sources were probably oral. They were not woven together in
a "scissors and paste" fashion; rather, they flowed or melted into
each other in oral form. Hence, some texts are a synthesis of several traditions in an indistinguishable form.

Sources

The existence of such sources was intuited on the basis of doublets, accounts that duplicate each other. The classic example is the "endangering of the ancestress" story that occurs in Gen 12:10–20; Gen 20:1–18; and Gen 26:6–11 wherein the patriarch calls his wife a sister and nearly loses her. Other doublets include Hagar cast out into the wilderness (Gen 16:1–16; Gen 21:8–21), covenant made with Abram/Abraham (Gen 12:1–9; Gen 15:1–21; Gen 17:1–27), and Moses striking a rock for water (Exod 17:1–7; Num 20:1–13). The slight differences in these obviously similar accounts probably led the final author or editor to include such duplicated accounts. Presumably, stories like this were collected by editors from various parts of the country (hence the differences in the accounts) and woven into oral cycles. The "sources" were probably oral cycles until they were woven together. When the cycles were merged to produce our biblical text, such duplications in the separate sources were evident in the final merged text that we now have. Thus, as you read the Bible you will encounter the same narrative in two or even three slightly different forms. The final editor respected all the accounts and retained them in the final comprehensive narrative. Sometimes two stories were merged with each other, such as Jacob's dream at Bethel in Gen 28, where one can separate two accounts: in one, God "stands" by Jacob; in the other, God is found atop the "ladder." As I've already noted, when there are two separate narratives that are duplicates, we call them doublets.

Such doublets were noticed already by Ibn-Ezra in the twelfth century, and he postulated that Moses had separate written sources at his disposal. Years later Martin Luther (1483–1546) and then Baruch Spinoza (1632–1677) made similar observations, but from the eighteenth century onward, scholars attempted to define what stories belonged to which biblical account. The modern theory as we would recognize it was provided by Julius Wellhausen in the 1880s.

The source-critical theory assumes that in the Pentateuch there are four strands that were woven together over the years to produce our final text: the Yahwist, the Elohist, the

11

Deuteronomists, and the Priestly editors. (Some scholars doubt the existence of the Elohist today, assuming it was really revisions added to the Yahwist.) The first two traditions are titled for names distinctively used for God (Yahweh and Elohim). It would be wrong, however, to think that the theory is built solely upon the use of the divine name, as some critics of the theory have maintained. The sources are identified by a complex of vocabulary, themes, and theology, which tend to occur together in stories from a given source on a recurring basis. The Yahwist and the Elohist sources appear to have pre-exilic, oral roots and were written down in the Babylonian exile (though scholars still debate this issue), while the Deuteronomists and Priestly editors generated written literature during the Babylonian exile (586–539 BCE) and beyond. The Priestly editors reworked both the Yahwist and the Elohist traditions by adding their own material. Their efforts produced the Pentateuch as we know it.

Method

The source critic proceeds by analyzing a text and observing the vocabulary and ideas that are particular to it. He or she then compares this with other texts that might share similar thought and language. For example, some accounts portray God as personal and in very physical terms, while others view God as transcendent. In the accounts of a transcendent God, revelation comes in dreams, by fire, by the angel of God, in a voice from heaven, or through prophets. The appearance the divine name Yahweh in the former texts and of the divine name Elohim in the latter texts may be observed regularly. Furthermore, the Yahwist accounts call the sacred mountain Sinai, and the inhabitants of the land are Canaanites; in the Elohist accounts the mountain is Horeb and the inhabitants of the land are Amorites. In addition to consistent use of different vocabulary, these separate sources regularly emphasize distinct theological values in their respective passages. So, for instance, early source critics suspected that two separate cycles of a given tale existed, and they noted that doublets often split these two cycles apart from each other and apart from the other two Pentateuchal traditions. Hence, the "source hypothesis" appeared convincing. It is important to recognize that sources are not divided according to a few random words, as some critics have said, but by numerous words and ideas that consistently occur together in the same sources. Sometimes when a source is isolated, particularly the Yahwist, the texts from a single source read more smoothly than the accepted, edited text does. When you isolate the Yahwist source and compare it with the Elohist source, which is extremely fragmentary, you will notice that the bulk of each narrative has a unique account, and in the edited text the occasional doublets (and synthesized texts) betray the once separate nature of the sources.

It must be noted that not all stories neatly separate. Obviously, certain accounts were told by all traditions in very similar fashion, which can make it difficult to assign some narratives to particular sources. For example, the Ten Commandments may have been found in at least two sources (Exod 20:2-17; Deut 5:6-21), and scholars have never agreed on their original context. Some accounts, like Gen 15 (God covenants with Abram) have been so tightly "melted" together from various sources that scholars cannot agree on their delineation. The sources in the Genesis flood narrative (Gen 6-8) and in Jacob's experience at Bethel (Gen 28:10-22) seem to separate more easily. But such is the nature of very fluid oral tradition, which was the original form of these "sources."

In the case of the stories about how the patriarch declares his wife to be his sister so that foreigners will not kill him to seize her, we have a more complex scenario with the three accounts in Gen 12:10-20; Gen 20:1-18; and Gen 26:6-11. We suspect that Gen 20:1-18 arose in the Elohist source, due to its particular vocabulary and the reference to a dream, while both Gen 12:10-20 and Gen 26:6-11 (which are duplicates of each other) were in the Yahwist source. The Yahwist obtained these two duplicate accounts, probably in oral form, but the differences in the two narratives caused the Yahwist to keep both in his epic source. As I've mentioned already, the Yahwist in particular reads more smoothly as a recreated narrative, if you isolate and bring all the narratives together associated with that source. The Elohist appears to be a collection of accounts placed into the Yahwist source at some point, either as a source that was dissected and mostly lost, or as an expansion or second edition of the Yahwist later on. (I prefer the first scenario.)

Purpose

The primary purpose of source criticism, as theoretical as it may be at times, is to isolate theology. With the different vocabulary and different themes, each source has a distinctive theology. Our present text is a symphony of harmonious sounds, as it were, when the four sources have been woven together, and the source critic wishes to isolate the particular instruments. The Yahwist, Elohist, Deuteronomists, and Priestly traditions each proclaimed a message to different generations—sometimes emphasizing forgiveness (Yahwist), at other times the need for repentance and obedience (Deuteronomists); sometimes portraying God as close and personal (Yahwist), and at other times distant and awesome (Elohist). To hear the message of one source clearly is to listen to the sermons of ancient preachers, for their purpose then was to interpret their intellectual heritage for their people, not merely to record antiquarian trivia. Their needs may be our needs at times, and their messages will come through more clearly to us when isolated. The result reminds us of the four Gospels, each of which tells us about the Jesus experience from a different community's perspective.

Source criticism is still a useful tool, especially for teaching students to discern theological nuances. But in many instances, scholars no longer use the method as it was practiced before 1930. Instead, much of the source-critical method has been taken up by form criticism and especially traditio-historical criticism.

Biblical Examples of Source Criticism

Genesis 28:10–18

The appearance of the LORD/God to Jacob at Bethel is a textbook example of two sources woven together by a biblical author or editor. It contains both Yahwist and Elohist traditions that nicely reflect the respective agendas of these two sources. It reads as follows:

> (10) Jacob left Beersheba and went toward Haran. (11) He came to a certain place and stayed there for the night, because the sun had set. Taking one of the stones of the place, he put it under his head and lay down in that place. (12) And he dreamed that there was a ladder set up on the earth, the top of it reaching to heaven; and the angels of God were ascending and descending on it. (13) And the LORD stood beside him and said, "I am the LORD, the God of Abraham your father and the God of Isaac; the land on which you lie I will give to you and to your offspring; (14) and your offspring shall be like the dust of the earth, and you shall spread abroad to the west and to the east and to the north and to the south; and all of the families of the earth shall be blessed in you and in your offspring. (15) Know that I am with you and will keep you wherever you go, and will bring you back to this land; for I will not leave you until I have done what I have promised you." (16) Then Jacob woke from his sleep and said, "Surely the LORD is in this place—and I did not know it!" (17) And he was afraid and said, "How awesome is this place! This is none other than the house of God, and this is the gate of heaven." (18) So Jacob rose early in the morning and he took the stone that he had put under his head and set it up for a pillar and poured oil on the top of it.

This narrative appears to be two separate narrative accounts that were very similar. Rather than preserving both accounts separately, as the final author of the text so often did, here the final biblical author sought to merge the two accounts together. Duplication of events in the narrative reflects the respect that the final biblical author had for both accounts.

A Short Introduction to Critical Old Testament Methodologies

Narrative A, which we shall call the Yahwist account, has the following characteristic traits:

1. The deity is portrayed in close and personal fashion, often next to the recipient of the revelation.

2. The sacred name for the deity is Yahweh, which we translate as LORD.

Narrative B, which we shall call the Elohist account, has the following characteristic traits:

1. The deity is distant and often speaks from the divine realm, not down on the ground.

2. The name for the deity is Elohim, which we translate as God.

3. The Elohist speaks of the fear of God and the awe that people should have before that deity.

4. The Elohist is interested in sacred stones, or *massebas*, and speaks of anointing things.

5. The Elohist is interested in dreams by which God can communicate to humans in a distant and respectful fashion. Dream reports are identified as such, and Elohist accounts reference the recipient of the revelation awakening in the morning to clearly indicate the revelation came in the recipient's sleep.

6. The Elohist often refers to the "angels of God," and sometimes the "angel of God" actually is God.

7. God sometimes speaks from the heavens in the Elohist. These themes occur in connection with each other, so that identification is not made on the basis of one theme.

So let us look at the chapter: Verse 10 is too vague to identify. Verse 11 uses the term *place*, a favorite word of the Elohist, and includes an allusion to sacred stones. Verse 12 refers to a dream, angels, and heaven, and it uses Elohim as the divine name—all traits typical of the Elohist. Verse 13 portrays the LORD as down on the earth next to Jacob, and uses the name Yahweh, typically Yahwist. Verses 14–15 flow from v. 13, so all three of these verses are Yahwist. Verse 16 uses the name Yahweh when Jacob awakes; it is Yahwist. Verse 17 refers to the fear of God, speaks of awe, mentions heaven, and use Elohim for God's name; it is Elohist. Verse 18 has Jacob awaken again, as he did in v. 16, but this is the Elohist version by virtue of the reference to sacred stones and anointing.

Dividing the verses in this passage by their sources was easier than in most of the Pentateuch, because often the final biblical author will melt two stories together like hot wax, making them difficult to separate. Also, it seems that in Gen 28, the author did leave out some parts of both stories in the merger process, but one can still read both narratives by themselves and they make sense as two separate accounts.

In other instances, the biblical author will inherit accounts from the two separate traditions and keep them separate if they are the same account but slightly different. In Gen 12 and 20 we have stories of Abraham passing his wife off as his sister. Gen 12 is Yahwist because the narrative is an its earthy recounting (Sarah goes into Pharaoh's harem), because the king is called "Pharaoh" (and not "the King of Egypt"), because the narrative features abrasive language, and because the deity is called the LORD. Gen 20 is Elohist because it has a dream report, because it portrays both Abimelech and Abraham respectfully, because Abraham only tells half a lie about Sarah as his sister, because Abraham and Abimelech speak piously to each other, because Sarah is not taken into the harem, because Abraham functions as a prophet (the Elohist likes prophets), because Abimelech makes reference to fear, and because the divine name Elohim is used. Both accounts are textbook examples of their respective sources; often in other comparable "melted" accounts the source delineation is not so clear.

The source critic separates out stories and portions of stories that belong to one source or another, and he or she can make observations about the theological perspective of the Yahwist and Elohist, once the sources have been separated. The Yahwist and the Elohist spoke to different ages with different religious needs, so the same memories are told differently in the separate sources. The final biblical author wove these larger collected sources (Yahwist and Elohist) together, often preserving duplicated accounts and also the duplications woven or melted together in individual accounts, out of respect for the received accounts. But that author did weave them together in a smooth and coherent fashion overall, and this editorial process of the final author is also a work of art (which sometimes makes it difficult for us to cleanly separate the sources). It is important to recognize that the modern source critic is really interested in the different theologies reflected in these various sources because these theologies tell us much about the overall religious perspective of ancient Israel.

Genesis 6:5—8:22

This much longer narrative is also a classic example of sources merged together: the Yahwist and the Priestly source or Priestly editors. Scholars debate whether the Priestly materials were an independent source merged with the other sources or whether they were editorial materials which drew the other sources together. If the Priestly material was a coherent and independent narrative before being woven together with the Yahwist here in the flood narrative, this is the opposite of what appears to be the case with Priestly texts elsewhere in the Pentateuch, where they appear as editorial additions. This is why some scholars (often Americans) speak of the Priestly editors and other scholars (often Germans) speak of the Priestly source. Over the flood narrative there is an additional debate as to whether the Yahwist narrative had Priestly texts added to it, or whether the Priestly narrative is an account supplemented by Yahwist narratives (Bailey 150; Blenkinsopp 77–87). This latter option might imply that the Priestly source is older than the Yahwist source, which is the opposite of what the overall source theory proposes. This debate will continue for years.

The following paragraphs are selections taken from my book *Misunderstood Stories*: (2014:200–216).

The reason for positing that two narratives exist is the presence of duplications in the overall story: (1) People are said to be sinful: 6:5 (J), 6:12 (P). (2) The coming of the flood is announced:

7:4 (J), 6:13, 17 (P). (3) Noah is ordered into the ark: 7:1–3 (J), 6:18–20 (P). (4) Noah obeys this directive: 7:5 (J), 6:22 (P). (5) Noah enters the ark: 7:7 (J), 7:13 (P). (6) The flood begins: 7:12 (J), 7:11 (P). (7) The floodwaters increase: 7:17 (J), 7:20–21 (P). (8) The floodwaters abate: 8:3a (J), 8:1 (P). (9) The promise of no more flood is given: 8:20–22 (J), 9:11–17 (P).

In addition, there are details that portray events differently, although in their final narrative synthesis they do not appear contradictory. These include: (1) Animals come in pairs, 6:19–20; 7:15–16 (P); clean animals come in seven pairs, 7:2 (J). (2) The flood is caused by rain, 7:4, 12; 8:2b (J); the flood is caused by the breaking of the "fountains of the deep" and the "firmament," a reversal of creation on day two of Gen 1 and a return to the chaos that existed before God began to create the world, 7:11; 8:2a (P). (3) The flood lasts forty days, 7:4, 12 (J); the flood lasts one year 8:13 (P). (4) According to 8:5 the mountains appear (P), but later according to 8:9 the waters still cover the earth (J). (5) Noah discovers the flood is ended from the response of the birds in 8:6, 12, 13b (J), but in 8:14–16 God informs him (P). (6) According to J, after forty days of rain (7:4, 12) the waters endure upon the earth for sixty-one days (7:10; 8:8–12); according the P the flood lasts for 150 days (7:24; 8:2a, 3b) and the waters do not recede until after one year (8:13a). (7) J texts in 6:5–7; 7:2; 8:21 allude to language in Gen 2–3, such as the words for "dirt" and "form," which are Yahwist in origin; P texts in 6:12, 20–21; 7:11, 17–21; 8:1–2; 9:1–3, 6–7 allude to words such as "seeing," "divine wind," "image of God," "rule" (over the animals), and "be fruitful and multiply" from Gen 1, which is Priestly in origin. (8) In 6:18 P alludes to the covenant, but J has no such reference. (9) Generally, J uses Yahweh (the English translation is LORD) for the name of God; P uses Elohim (the English translation is God). (10) P often uses language from Gen 1 to describe the animals (6:20; 7:14, 16, 21; 8:17, 19) and refers to provisioning the animals (6:21; 9:2–3) (Skinner 164; Vawter 115; Bailey 149–50; Carr 64–65). Obviously, the biblical author who created the final text respected both accounts and wove them together rather well.

Thus, the J narrative is reconstructed as follows: Gen 6:5–8; 7:1–5, 7–10, 12, 16b–17, 22–23; 8:2b–3a, 6–12, 13b, 20–22. The P narrative is reconstructed as follows: Gen 6:9–22; 7:6, 11, 13–16a, 18–21, 24; 8:1, 2a, 3b–5, 13a, 14–19; 9:1–17. We shall make occasional references to these divisions when it is theologically significant. In the following narrative the Yahwist source is indicated by regular print and the Priestly source or editing is indicated by italicized print.

Genesis 6:5–22

(5) The LORD saw that the wickedness of humankind was great in the earth, and that every inclination of the thoughts of their hearts was only evil continually. (6) And the LORD was sorry that he had made humankind on the earth, and it grieved him to his heart. (7) So the LORD said, "I will blot out from the earth the human beings I have created—people together with animals and creeping things and birds of the air, for I am sorry that I have made them." (8) But Noah found favor in the sight of the LORD.

(9) *These are the descendants of Noah. Noah was a righteous man, blameless in his generation; Noah walked with God. (10) And Noah had three sons, Shem, Ham, and Japheth.*

(11) *Now the earth was corrupt in God's sight, and the earth was filled with violence. (12) And God saw that the earth was corrupt; for all flesh had corrupted its ways upon the earth. (13) And God said to Noah, "I have determined to make an end of all flesh, for the earth is filled with violence because of them; now I am going to destroy them along with the earth. (14) Make yourself an ark of cypress wood; make rooms in the ark, and cover it inside and out with pitch. (15) This is how you are to make it: the length of the ark three hundred cubits, its width fifty cubits, and its height thirty cubits. (16) Make a roof for the ark, and finish it to a cubit above; and put the door of the ark in its side; make it with lower, second, and third decks.*

(17) *For my part, I am going to bring a flood of waters on the earth, to destroy from under heaven all flesh in which is the breath of life; everything that is on the earth shall die.* (18) *But I will establish my covenant with you; and you shall come into the ark, you, your sons, your wife, and your sons' wives with you.* (19) *And of every living thing, of all flesh, you shall bring two of every kind into the ark, to keep them alive with you; they shall be male and female.* (20) *Of the birds according to their kinds, and of the animals according to their kinds, of every creeping thing of the ground according to its kind, two of every kind shall come in to you, to keep them alive.* (21) *Also take with you every kind of food that is eaten, and store it up; and it shall serve as food for you and for them."* (22) *Noah did this; he did all that God commanded him.*

(One should note that Gen 6:7 is a Yahwist text which uses the name LORD, while Gen 1 is a Priestly text. If the Yahwist knows the Priestly text, this is a good argument for the priority of the Priestly tradition over the Yahwist tradition.)

Beginning with v. 9 we have what almost appears to be another introduction, and with the switch from the word LORD to the word God, commentators suggest that there was a seam or division between vv. 8 and 9—the division between the Yahwist and the Priestly sources. But with the use of the name God previously in v. 5, this theory is rendered tenuous, because v. 5 flows logically into vv. 6–8. Thus, v. 5 should go with vv. 9 onward due to the use of the divine name, but it fits with the plot in vv. 6–8. Perhaps the editorial process for this narrative is more complex than we can reconstruct by simply observing the final product. Biblical authors are artists, not just brick masons, laying sources next to each other mechanically. The sources used by the biblical authors are created, changed, and woven together. At any rate, the narrative continues with the name God, and the plot appears somewhat to be a parallel version to what was recounted in v. 5–8, yet the division is not clean enough to be convincing to all commentators.

The language again reminds us of Gen 1–2. Verse 17 refers to the "breath of life," an expression in Gen 2:7 given to humanity, but here it is an attribute of all creatures. Verse 20 repeats the reference to cattle and creeping things of day six in Gen 1. Verse 21 refers to the food to be taken on board for people and animals, and we receive the impression that it is grain. So does this imply that the animals are vegetarian? It is difficult to say! Verse 18 foreshadows the Priestly covenant that God will make with Noah after the flood.

Genesis 7:1–24

(1) Then the LORD said to Noah, "Go into the ark, you and all your household, for I have seen that you alone are righteous before me in this generation. (2) Take with you seven pairs of all clean animals, the male and its mate; and a pair of the animals that are not clean, the male and its mate; (3) and seven pairs of the birds of the air also, male and female, to keep their kind alive on the face of all the earth. (4) For in seven days I will send rain on the earth for forty days and forty nights; and every living thing that I have made I will blot out from the face of the ground." (5) And Noah did all that the LORD had commanded him.

(6) *Noah was six hundred years old when the flood of waters came on the earth.* (7) And Noah with his sons and his wife and his sons' wives went into the ark to escape the waters of the flood. (8) Of clean animals, and of animals that are not clean, and of birds, and of everything that creeps on the ground, (9) *two and two, male and female, went into the ark with Noah, as God had commanded Noah.* (10) And after seven days the waters of the flood came on the earth.

(11) *In the six hundredth year of Noah's life, in the second month, on the seventeenth day of the month, on that day all the fountains of the great deep burst forth, and windows of the heavens were opened.* (12) The rain fell on the earth forty days and forty nights. (13) *On the very same day Noah with his sons, Shem and Ham and Japheth, and Noah's wife and the three wives of his sons entered the ark,* (14) *they and every wild animal of every kind, and all domestic animals of every kind, and every*

creeping thing that creeps on the earth, and every bird of every kind—every bird, every winged creature. (15) *They went into the ark with Noah, two and two of all flesh in which there was the breath of life.* (16) *And those that entered, male and female of all flesh, went in as God had commanded him; and the Lord shut him in.*

(17) The flood continued forty days on the earth; and the waters increased, and bore up the ark, and it rose high above the earth. (18) *The waters swelled and increased greatly on the earth; and the ark floated on the face of the waters.* (19) *The waters swelled so mightily on the earth that all the high mountains under the whole heaven were covered;* (20) *the waters swelled above the mountains, covering them fifteen cubits deep.* (21) *And all flesh died that moved on the earth, birds, domestic animals, wild animals, all swarming creatures that swarm on the earth, and all human beings;* (22) everything on dry land in whose nostrils was breath of life died. (23) He blotted out every living thing that was on the face of the ground, human beings and animals and creeping things and birds of the air; they were blotted out from the earth. Only Noah was left, and those that were with him in the ark. (24) *And the waters swelled on the earth for one hundred fifty days.*

The LORD gives Noah directions in vv. 1–4 that parallel the directions given in chapter 6. Commentators have been tempted to call these passages part of the Yahwist tradition, especially since the reference is now to the LORD rather than to God, as was the case with Gen 6:14–22.

What really stands out are the directions for the animals. Now Noah is commanded to take seven pairs of clean animals and one pair of unclean animals. We assume that there were seven pairs of clean animals for food consumption by the humans and the other animals. The reference to seven pairs of every clean animal tempts us into making source divisions of the narrative. Since Priestly traditions attribute the categories of clean and unclean animals to Mosaic legislation, they would not introduce the concept here in the flood narrative. Hence, scholars have suggested that these are Yahwist texts (and the name LORD occurs here). However, one wonders why the Yahwist would have this theme in the flood narrative when the concept of clean and unclean animals occurs nowhere else in Yahwist texts. Nevertheless, commentators assume these are Yahwist texts. (I am suspicious.) Commentators also point out that since the post-flood narratives speak of God giving permission for meat consumption to people, the residents on the ark would not have been able to eat meat, if indeed that was the purpose of the extra animals. Thus, in an overall assessment commentators suspect that the directions given to Noah in Gen 6:14–22 are Priestly and the directions in Gen 7:1–4 are Yahwist. Was our final editor of these narratives so inept as to put in both sets of directions, which appear to contradict each other? No! This editor may have respected both sets of tradition and felt that they could be viewed as complementary, not contradictory. The directions given by God at first in chapter 6 were to be seen as simply undergoing further clarification by the later directions in chapter 7.

In 7:4 we are told that the LORD would cause it to rain for forty days. This Yahwist text will be complemented by Priestly information of a symbolic nature in later verses.

In vv. 5–10 we are informed that Noah did as he was commanded by the LORD and took in the clean and unclean animals.

In v. 4 Noah was told that it would rain, but in v. 11 the flood is described in a more destructive manner. This latter verse, which appears to be Priestly in origin, describes how the foundations of the deep broke apart and the waters below the earth came up and met the waters falling down from the heavens. We are reminded of Gen 1 where God separated the waters above the firmament from the waters below the firmament. In effect, creation was undone and the world returned to its primordial state. Thus, this Priestly text refers back to the Priestly text in Gen 1.

Verse 13 of chapter 7 mentions Noah's three sons by name. It is the second such reference to them. Previously they were named in Gen 6:10, another Priestly text. It is interesting to observe that they parallel Lamech's three sons, a narrative from the Yahwist tradition. Lamech's three sons provide the world with civilization; Noah's three sons provide the world with its people. Does the contrast of interest between civilization and propagation somehow reflect the difference between the Yahwist historian and the Priestly editors?

Verse 16 mentions that after Noah and the animals went into the ark that the "LORD shut him in" (either a strange interruption of the Priestly narrative by the Yahwist, or the beginning of Yahwist material). What an interesting observation—the LORD closed the door on the ark! Did Noah forget to put a door handle on the inside of the ark, so the LORD had to close it for him? We suspect that this is one of those images provided by the Yahwist tradition to speak of the LORD being intimately involved in the process with the human creation. It also contrasts vividly with the Mesopotamian flood narratives wherein the gods become terrified of the tremendous power of the flood they unleashed. In the biblical narrative the LORD is in control of the flood and the ark throughout the entire experience, closing the ark's door and guiding the ark until it comes to rest on the mountain.

Genesis 8:1–22

(1) *But God remembered Noah and all the wild animals and all the domestic animals that were with him in the ark. And God made a wind blow over the earth, and the waters subsided;* (2) *the fountains of the deep and the windows of the heavens were closed,* the rain from the heavens was restrained, (3) and the waters gradually receded from the earth. *At the end of one hundred fifty days the waters had abated;* (4) *and in the seventh month, on the seventeenth day of the month, the ark came to rest on the mountains of Ararat.* (5) *The waters continued to abate until the tenth month; in the tenth month, on the first day of the month, the tops of the mountains appeared.*

(6) At the end of forty days Noah opened the window of the ark that he had made (7) and sent out the raven; and it went to and fro until the waters were dried up from the earth. (8) Then he sent out the dove from him, to see if the waters had subsided from the face of the

ground; (9) but the dove found no place to set its foot; and it returned to him to the ark, for the waters were still on the face of the whole earth. So he put out his hand and took it and brought it into the ark with him. (10) He waited another seven days, and again he sent out the dove from the ark; (11) and the dove came back to him in the evening, and there in its beak was a freshly plucked olive leaf; so Noah knew that the waters had subsided from the earth. (12) Then he waited another seven days, and sent out the dove; and it did not return to him any more.

(13) *In the six hundred first year, in the first month, the first day of the month, the waters dried up from the earth;* and Noah removed the covering of the ark, and looked, and saw that the face of the ground was drying. (14) *In the second month, on the twenty-seventh day of the month, the earth was dry.* (15) *Then God said to Noah,* (16) *"Go out of the ark, you and your wife, and your sons and your sons' wives with you.* (17) *Bring out with you every living thing that is with you of all flesh—birds and animals and every creeping thing that creeps on the earth—so that they may abound on the earth, and be fruitful and multiply on the earth."* (18) *So Noah went out with his sons and his wife and his sons' wives.* (19) *And every animal, every creeping thing, and every bird, everything that moves on the earth, went out of the ark by families.*

(20) The Noah built an altar to the LORD, and took of every clean animal and of every clean bird, and offered burnt offerings on the altar. (21) And when the LORD smelled the pleasing odor, the LORD said in his heart, "I will never again curse the ground because of human-kind, for the inclination of the human heart is evil from youth; nor will I ever again destroy every living creature as I have done.

(22) As long as the earth endures,
seedtime and harvest, cold and heat,
summer and winter, day and night,
shall not cease."

It is fascinating to observe the similarities between the creation account and the flood account, especially with the addition of material from the Priestly editors, who sought to portray the flood as the direct undoing of the creation according to Gen 1.

In both narratives we have chaotic waters and references to the firmament and the fountains of the deep. As the flood comes to a closure, the divine wind moves upon the face of the water, the water and land separate, mountains appear, fresh growth arises on trees, and eventually animals leave the ark and appear on the land (Wenham 207). It is another classic example of how biblical authors loved to make their various narratives appear like other narratives (intertextuality).

In the first five verses of chapter 8 we are introduced to new aspects of the flood timetable. Scholars have assumed that the Yahwist chronology is one of forty days of rain, while the Priestly chronology is one of a yearlong chaotic flood. The final author or editor of these narratives reconciles these chronologies with the scenario that it rained for forty days and floodwaters endured on the earth for a year. The reference to forty days in v. 6 is odd, since by this time the ark had been afloat for over half a year. One good suggestion is that in the original Yahwist narrative it meant after the forty days of rain had stopped. Once Priestly material was added to the Yahwist narrative, then this became simply another period of time in the yearlong flood chronology to be seen as different from the initial forty days of rain. If so, this is evidence that the Yahwist tradition is prior to the Priestly tradition.

God tells Noah to disembark from the ark. All of the animals come out; there is no reference to the seven pairs of clean animals. In v. 20 the name of the deity changes to the LORD, and the reference to the clean animals occurs again, evidence for some readers that this is a Yahwist text.

In v. 22 the Yahwist account of the flood ends with a little poem in which the LORD promises the stability of the seasons. This complements v. 21 in which the LORD promises never to flood the earth again. Such a promise flies in the face of Mesopotamian beliefs that fear the possibility of a chaotic flood in the spring of every year, which necessitates devotion and sacrifice to Marduk. This is a powerful biblical polemic with which to conclude the flood story. However, the Priestly editors will provide a grand conclusion to the flood narrative, a covenant between God and Noah (and the rest of humanity, too) in Gen 9.

The flood narrative is a good portion of the text upon which to practice the source-critical approach. Some other texts are more difficult. Often our best textbook examples are in the book of Genesis. The source-critical theory has problems, but not enough to dissuade scholars from using it, even if in various modified forms. But it is helpful entry into the study of the biblical text.

3

FORM CRITICISM

As a discipline, Form Criticism emerged in Old Testament studies through the efforts of scholars such as Hermann Gunkel (1862–1932), Hugo Gressmann (1877–1927), Sigmund Mowinckel (1884–1965) (a student of Gunkel), Johannes Pedersen (1883–1977), Ivan Engnell (1906–1964), and others in the 1920s and 1930s. Form critics seek to analyze one particular passage in order to discern its structure, genre, and the original setting in Israelite life whence it came. Form criticism emerged because many exegetes were unimpressed with the results of source criticism in particular parts of the Bible, and they wished to turn their attention more directly to the consideration of individual texts. The discipline has been most fruitful in the consideration of the Psalms, where we find clearly defined texts that can sustain isolated study. Gunkel's pioneering studies in form criticism addressed material in the Psalms and Genesis, and Mowinckel also gave attention to the Psalms.

Form critics tend to focus on the oral transmission of a passage over the years. The oral tradition comes from the life of the people, so that as one critic noted, form criticism is interested to a greater extent in the total life of the people. Form critics believe that while source critics focus on the meaning of the passage at one particular stage of development, form critics observe how the text evolved in the life of the people and had different meanings over the years. Oral literature was told in the family, in the villages, in the royal court, in many places where people were to be found. Thus, the transmission of a particular narrative may involve a long and complicated history, involving the lives of people and social institutions, which we can never fully discover. But to engage in a quest to understand how and where a story evolved in oral form can lead the scholar to many insights, even if they are hypothetical. In its final form the oral literature precipitates into written form at some point, and this is where the task of the source critic or the traditio-historical critic takes over. A very thorough history of form criticism in the broadest sense (from the ancient church onward), and scholarship related to it, was written by Martin Buss (Buss 1999).

Methods

How does a form critic proceed in analyzing a biblical text? First, the reader must determine the extent of the text: where does it begin and end, and is it internally coherent or unified? With the various psalms or an individual proverb this is easy; the unit is self-evident. In narrative or prophetic oracles, the reader must ascertain where the unit clearly begins and ends. Often certain stereotypical formulas or the plot may help the determination.

Second, the reader may determine the internal structure or outline of the literary unit. Since most Hebrew literature was communicated in oral and poetic form, our biblical material often has a discernible structure with some harmonic balance to the various parts. Readers will discover that certain patterns or conventionally stereotyped phrases tend to recur in several texts. This makes identification easy and leads to the next step of identifying the literature.

Third, the reader may classify the form according to its genre; that is, it may be similar in structure and content to a number of other texts. There may be a standard literary type the author could have used on the occasion for which this biblical text was generated. When scholars speak of a "form" in form criticism, they sometimes mean the overall shape of a text, but usually they are speaking of the literary category to which a particular text belongs.

For example, there are particular ways of articulating a lament psalm, thanksgiving psalm, judgment oracle, hope oracle, prophetic call narrative, or dream report; these are some of the many well-established literary types. The reader of a text may identify the category or form/genre to which his or her text belongs.

It is worth saying that there are two meanings to the word "form." One is the shape of the text, the internal outlines it displays. *Formgeschichte* is the word used by Germans to describe this quest. The other meaning of the word is "genre" or type of literature the text is. *Gattungsgeschichte* is the word the Germans used to describe this task. English hampers us a little bit by using "form" to describe both concepts.

Fourth, the reader may seek to hypothesize the original setting (the German term was *Sitz im Leben*) for which a literary unit was used, whether in the cult (that is, in worship), in intellectual circles, in the royal court, in prophetic groups, or elsewhere. The questions one must ask are these: Where was the form used, and what did it mean for those people? Usually, the original setting was one in which the biblical material was orally communicated. In addition, the form critic may determine not only the original "life-setting" but also the initial shape of the material. Sometimes texts have additions made to them over the years, as they are applied to new situations, and this will cause texts to take on new meanings. The form critic seeks to discover the original meaning of a given text and to hypothesize about its development and about further meanings imparted it.

Finally, the reader doing form criticism seeks to recover the fuller meaning of a passage. What did the text say in its original oral setting, and what later meanings were imparted to it in the developmental process? What did it mean when it finally came into the written canon where we now observe it? Most importantly, what does it now say to us after we have recovered some of its original meaning? This last stage is the theological task, often engaged in by a preacher who seeks to find deep meaning in the pericope for the modern congregation.

Types

Over the years form critics have identified a number of "forms" of genres in biblical literature. Although every textbook will differ in its typology of forms, the following is a representative list:

Songs

Among the various types of psalms there are lament hymns, thanksgiving hymns, hymns of praise, torah liturgies, wisdom psalms, pilgrimage hymns, royal hymns, and enthronement hymns. In the early years of Israel, hymns may have been sung at festivals by Israelites both at shrines and in their village communities. In later years the hymns that became the psalms most likely were sung at the temple in Jerusalem by priests and Levites regularly, and by laypeople at special occasions or festivals. We really have to make educated guesses as to the settings in which psalms were used.

To call a psalm a hymn is to define its genre, and to identify the internal parts of a psalm is to describe its form or shape. Thus, a lament hymn will have an invocation, remembrance of God's graciousness in the past, lament (complaint about God's actions, personal affliction, and/or actions of enemies), petition, protestation of innocence, affirmation of the petitioner's intent to praise God if deliverance occurs, and doxology. Form can help define genre.

Laws

There are two broad types of legal formulations in the biblical material, each with many variations. *Apodictic* laws state a command absolutely, as though it came directly from God ("you shall" or "you shall not" or "cursed be one who"), and *casuistic* laws state a situation and the punishment that should follow, as if an example is being given to judges for their deliberation in a courtroom. ("If thus and such is the crime, then this should be the punishment.") Casuistic laws are the most common in the written ancient Near

Eastern law codes that we have, such as the codes of Ur-Nammu of Ur (2050 BCE), Lipit-Ishtar of Isin (1850 BCE), and Hammurabi of Babylon (1750 BCE), as well as many others.

Prophetic Oracles

Oracles are little poems that can announce doom/judgment or hope/salvation. They were spoken in public by a prophet who wished to communicate a religious message to the people. A prophet might have proclaimed any such oracle in the "form" of a parable, courtroom accusation, funeral dirge, or any other conventional pattern for speaking in everyday life. (Despite variations in form, the genre of such a pronouncement is consistently the prophetic oracle.) Furthermore, prophetic literature also provides us with prophetic call narratives, prayers, and prophetic biographies. These oracles might have been remembered in oral form for a generation (for example those of Jeremiah) or for many years (for example those of Amos and Hosea). Many oracles of the pre-exilic prophets may have been written down during the sixth-century BCE Babylonian exile.

Wisdom or Didactic Literature

Herein we find the well-known proverb as well as less frequent "forms" like the riddle, parable, and allegory; we also find debate formats (the entire book of Job), short stories, and hymns. Wisdom literature often addressed everyday issues of life and provided advice on how to be successful. Some biblical wisdom literature, however, did address religious issues, such as divine order in the world, creation, and the reason for suffering. These themes are typical of the later wisdom literature (Prov 1–9, the books of Sirach and Wisdom of Solomon). In general, wisdom literature has the greatest parallels with ancient Near Eastern extrabiblical literature: proverbs are found in Egypt, and Joban laments are found in Mesopotamia.

Narrative

The various types here are more difficult to distinguish, but most scholars identify the following: chronicles or royal annals, legends, sagas, historical romances or short stories, novellas, myths, fables, and fairy tales. (Remember that a literary classification in no way passes judgment on whether a text is inspired by God, true or false, or religiously meaningful; nor does such categorization comment on whether the events described happened in actual history.) Critics seek to identify the forms chosen by the biblical authors to communicate their messages. Within these broader types, various scholars propose many subtypes depending upon their analysis of the texts.

Once the literary genre or form of a text has been identified, the reader discovers additional levels of meaning in the text. Biblical texts speak to us by both their content and literary form. The literary medium is also part of the message. In the ancient world, even more so than today, an audience gleaned much of the message communicated by an author, when they recognized the stereotypical language of a particular genre. If an author failed to use a clear genre in his literary work, he might run the risk of confusing and losing the audience. Use of a formula was as important as the actual words of the message; the "form" communicated.

Biblical Examples of Form Criticism

Two texts are worthy of our consideration. The first tells the experience of young Samuel in 1 Sam 3, which will be explicated as an ancient Near Eastern auditory message dream. The second text will be far more simple. The component parts of a lament hymn will be evaluated.

1 Samuel 3:1–18

As an example of form-critical analysis I have drawn upon some of the text from my article "A Reconsideration of the Form-Critical

Structure in I Samuel 3: An Ancient Near Eastern Dream Theophany," in *Zeitschrift für die alttestamentliche Wissenschaft* 94 (1982) 379–90. In this article I suggest that Samuel's experience at Shiloh is portrayed by the biblical author as an auditory message dream revelation and not as a prophetic call experience. Thus, I do two form-critical analyses of the text, one as a dream revelation and the other as a prophetic call experience. I also do both examples of form-critical analysis: I seek to identity the genre of the passage, and I outline the component form-critical parts of the passage.

The account in 1 Sam 3 need not be reproduced here, for it is a well-known and oft-recited story. Commentators often entitle the narrative as the prophetic call of Samuel and see it in connection with prophetic calls of Moses, Isaiah, Jeremiah, and Ezekiel. But they do not undertake a detailed form-critical evaluation of the narrative as such. (Some scholars who have written commentaries on 1 Samuel starting in the 1990s and thereafter have told me that my article convinced them that this chapter is a dream report.)

A. Leo Oppenheim (1904–1974) generated a classification of ancient Near Eastern dreams and the discernment of the literary genre for recording dream theophanies in the ancient texts (Oppenheim). In his classification he suggests the following types: (1) *auditory message dreams*, wherein the recipient hears a message from the god but sees no imagery; (2) *symbolic message dreams*, where the recipient sees a vision and hears no voice from the deity (though a voice is heard in some instances); and (3) *psychological status dreams*, which are the dreams of everyday people, often frenetic, which require interpretation. The first two types are revelatory dream experiences that come to important people, such as rulers and priests, and are literary creations by scribes for the political purposes of those kings and priests. The last category probably reflects the real dream experiences of people, which dream interpreters and dream books exist to decode, in order for the dreamer to remove the impurity that such a dream might bring.

Oppenheim outlines the format of auditory message dreams as follows:

I. Setting

   A. Who—dream recipient

   B. When—the time of the dream

   C. Where—the site, usually a shrine

   D. Conditions—circumstances surrounding dream reception

II. Dream Content—report of the visual imagery in a symbolic message dream or the spoken message in an auditory message dreams

III. Termination of the Dream—statement that the dreamer awoke and realized it was a dream

IV. Fulfillment of the Dream—account of how the words of the deity came true

With Oppenheim's categories we may observe the component parts of an auditory message dream report in 1 Sam 3. Verses 1–4a describe the setting of the dream theophany; Samuel is the recipient; the site is Shiloh, a holy sanctuary; the time is at night, perhaps just before dawn; and the various circumstances are given to prepare the audience for the message of the deity. Verses 11–14 contain the message of the deity. Verse 15a contains the termination of the dream theophany, which is indicated by the detail that Samuel lay until morning.

An abbreviated comparison with ancient Near Eastern parallels shows how the Samuel narrative form-critically corresponds to the ancient Near Eastern auditory message dream format.

(1) *Setting in a shrine.* "Samuel was lying down in the temple of the LORD, where the ark of God was" (v. 2). In Ugaritic dreams Keret and Dan'el are in special rooms to incubate a theophany. The priest of Ashurbanipal, the Assyrian king, was in a shrine. Pharaoh Thutmosis IV was in the shadow of the sphinx.

(2) *Recipient is asleep.* "Samuel was lying down in the temple of the LORD" (v. 3). Mesopotamian dreams indicate that the king rested. Assyrian dreams in particular say the king was in bed. "Prince Bekhten slept in his bed." "Sleep took hold of Thutmosis"

Form Criticism

IV. The Chaldean king Nabonidus received his dream in the part of the night meant for sleep. Ugaritic Keret cried himself to sleep, and Dan'el lay down to sleep.

(3) *Reference to time.* Samuel was there, and "the lamp of God had not yet gone out" (v. 3), at the time before dawn when the oil was consumed. The Akkadian word for "dream" implies early morning sleep. Chaldean king Nabonidus receives his dream when all men are said to be asleep.

(4) *Recipient awakened for theophany.* The LORD calls to Samuel three times. Ashurbanipal's priest was awakened by Ishtar to receive a night vision. At Ugarit, Keret was awakened and startled. The Egyptian word for "dream" is related to the verb "to be startled," and the hieroglyph is an open eye. Commentators err when they say Samuel is not dreaming due to his waking state, because that is the literary convention of these dream reports.

(5) *Introductory formula.* When the recipient is awake, the deity will utter an exclamation, an imperative, or rhetorical questions. Samuel hears the LORD call his name. Ishtar says to Ashurbanipal, "Be not afraid!" Ishtar says to Hattushilish the Hittite, "Shall I abandon you to a hostile deity? Be not afraid!" El says to Keret at Ugarit, "What ails Keret that he weeps?"

(6) *Self-identification of the deity.* Thutmosis IV hears, "I am your father Harmakhis-Khepri-Re-Atum," and Pharaoh Djoser hears, "I am Khnum, your fashioner." Yahweh is identified for Samuel by Eli.

(7) *Visual apparition* (sometimes). "The LORD came and stood there" (v. 10) for Samuel, which may imply a visual apparition. Ishtar says to Ashurbanipal, "Be not afraid that you see me!" The Sumerian ruler Eannatum had the deity appear by his head. Ashurbanipal's priest says that the deity came into the room and then left afterward. In the dreams of Nabonidus, the Chaldean king, Marduk stood before him once, a man stood beside him once, and the god Sin appeared in all his glory in another dream. Pharaoh Djoser says the god stood beside him. Pharaoh Merneptah saw the god Ptah. The deity tells Pharaoh Thutmosis IV to look at him. At Ugarit, Keret's dream reports that the god El approached.

(8) *Message.* The LORD delivers a word of judgment against the Elides in vv. 10–14. In ancient Near Eastern dreams the deity usually asks the king or the priest to do something, such as build a temple. Thutmosis IV has to clear the sand away from the sphinx. Ishtar promises to lead Ashurbanipal in battle, and Sin promises Ashurbanipal victory in battle. The wife of Hattushilish the Hittite hears that Ishtar will help her husband. Keret receives the promise of a son.

(9) *Human response.* Samuel says, "Speak, for your servant is listening" (v. 10). Nabonidus argues with both Sin and Marduk that he cannot rebuild a temple up in Haran because the enemy holds the city. Hattushilis in two of his several dreams tells Lady Danu Hepa about his votive offerings.

(10) *Termination of dream with reference that the recipient was asleep.* Verse 15 says that Samuel "lay there until morning." In Akkadian dreams, the recipient "awakens with a start." Tanutamon "awoke and kissed the earth." Pharaoh Djoser says, "I awoke refreshed." Pharaoh Thutmosis IV says he awoke and recognized the words of the god. Keret awoke and realized that it was a dream.

All of these parallels, some of which are clearer than others, indicate that the experience of Samuel is being portrayed as a dream by the biblical author, in particular as an auditory message dream. So we should form-critically define it as such. But first we must consider the other form-critical option vying for our attention.

Over the years most commentators have considered this text to be the prophetic call experience of Samuel. But does it really have the component parts of a prophetic call narrative as we find elsewhere in the biblical text? The most thorough evaluation of the prophetic call narrative format was provided by Norman Habel (Habel 1965). He delineates the following components: (1) divine confrontation—the Lord comes in a theophany, (2) introductory word—the Lord calls the recipient and provides a divine self-identification, (3) commission—the Lord gives the recipient his prophetic calling and instructions, (4) prophetic denial—the prophet declares his unworthiness or limitations to be a prophet, (5) reassurance—the Lord overturns the prophet's objections to the call, (6) sign—the prophet receives a physical demonstration of the reality of the call.

When we turn to the Samuel account, we see that it has some of these elements, but not all. The first two elements are present when the LORD comes to Samuel and calls his name. But these are elements common to many different theophanic experiences (including dream reports). The important omission in Samuel's experience is the prophetic commission. Furthermore, the encounter between the LORD and Samuel lacks an objection by Samuel to his prophetic calling, nor is there divine reassurance and a sign of the prophetic calling. Much is missing. Defenders of Samuel's prophetic call find these elements in the ensuing narrative. Samuel's reluctance to relate the divine message to Eli is construed as Samuel's objection to the prophetic call, Eli's encouragement to speak is supposedly the divine reassurance, and Samuel's continuing ministry is the sign of the prophetic calling.

Stretching the elements of the prophetic call format to these narrative elements stretches the call narrative structure too far. The prophetic call narrative is an encounter between God and the prophet. That the prophetic objection and the divine reassurance occur in the encounter between God and the prophet is the testimony that the prophet has been truly called by God. Transferal of these categories to a human-to-human encounter vitiates that theological emphasis. To receive assurance from Eli undermines the authority of divine reassurance and destroys the heart of the call narrative, which is an encounter with God in dramatic fashion. The sign is witness to this call and the encounter, so to make Samuel's subsequent ministry the sign loses the symbolism of the sign as testimony to the beginning of the prophetic ministry.

Therefore, it seems most appropriate to conclude that Samuel's experience cannot be defined as a prophetic call narrative, for it lacks too many of the constitutive elements. The experience of Samuel appears far more like an ancient Near Eastern auditory message dream theophany.

Psalm 13

Lament hymns in the Psalter are the most frequently encountered psalms. In a form-critical analysis, they have the most component parts that can theoretically appear. In a sense, the analysis of a lament hymn is not only easy but somewhat fun. The component parts do not all occur in any one psalm, but enough do in order to identify the genre. Nor do these component parts occur in the same sequence, but there is somewhat of an order that can be observed if you take enough lament psalms into consideration. What you look for in a lament hymn or psalm are the following elements: (1) invocation; (2) praise of God or remembrance of past graciousness; (3) lament, which comes in three types (complaint against God, complaint about self-suffering, and complaint about the "enemies" that persecute or ridicule the sufferer); (4) protestation of innocence; (5) petitions to God, often three in number, (6) confession of trust that God will act; (7) promise to praise God (often in the temple) if sufferer is delivered; and (8) doxology. A thanksgiving psalm will be defined as such because there is a reference to past suffering and a statement that this praise fulfills the promise to praise God in the lament psalm.

Ps 13 is a good test case for us, because it is short and has many of the elements listed above. Longer psalms may have more of the elements, but they will have a lot of other language not really part of the lament psalm format.

Ps 13:1–6: (1) How long, O LORD? Will you forget me forever? How long will you hide your face from me? (2) How long must I bear pain in my soul, and have sorrow in my heart all day long? How long shall my enemy be exalted over me? (3) Consider and answer me, O LORD my God! Give light to my eyes, or I will sleep the sleep of death (4) and my enemy will say, "I have prevailed"; my foes will rejoice because I am shaken. (5) But I have trusted in your steadfast love; my heart shall rejoice in your salvation. (6) I will sing to the LORD, because he has dealt bountifully with me.

There is no invocation. The psalm begins in v. 1 with complaint against God in the form of three questions (psalmists like phrases that come in threes). Verses 2a and 2b contain the lament about self-suffering. Verse 2c contains the lament about the enemies. Enemies may be foreign enemies, people who seek to hurt you, or friends who assume that your suffering is due to your sin. Verse 3 contains three verbs that are petitions: "consider," "answer," and "give light." They call upon God to act for the sufferer. Verse 4 is a more extensive reference to the enemies, who are vague in this psalm. Verse 5 is a confession of trust. Last of all, v. 6 is the promise to praise God if God helps the sufferer. Though this psalm is short, it has a lament with all three references (God, self, enemies), petition, confession of trust, and promise to praise God if delivered. These are the elements most important to a lament hymn, especially the elements of lament (God, self, enemies), without which, it would not be a lament hymn.

Lament hymns or psalms were flexible. Often the references in the lament are general enough to cover a host of situations. The lament hymns as well as the thanksgiving hymns occur both as hymns to be sung by individuals and hymns to be sung by groups. I have always suspected that the individual and the corporate psalms could become interchangeable with the modification of a few words. Such hymns provided people with a literary form, in this case, a song, by which they could express their deepest feelings, especially pain and sorrow. They enable people to scream at God in pain. For what is the expression of anger at God, if not truly prayer?

Form criticism analyzes the genre and form or shape of different pieces of literature. This stereotypical language that would identify a form for us also enabled the ancient Israelites to express themselves in established and well known language, be it in a hymn of lament, in simple praise, in thanksgiving, in a prophetic call narrative, or in a dream report.

Conclusion

Form criticism studies the outline of a piece of literature and identifies the genre or type of literature. Often discerning the outline will also identify the genre. This is particularly the case with the two examples considered above. Most significantly, the "form" communicates to the audience much of the message that the author wishes to convey.

4

TRADITIO-HISTORICAL CRITICISM

THIS METHOD OF ANALYSIS is called by several names, including the traditions history method or traditio-historical criticism, all of which are English translations of German terms, *Traditions-geschichtliche Studien* and *Überlieferungsgeschichtliche Studien*. In New Testament scholarship the preferred term is "redaction criticism," especially in reference to the critical evaluation of the Gospels. This diversity in nomenclature parallels the even greater range in approaches exhibited by individual scholars in their evaluation of particular texts. Thus, one must make a very broad definition of the method in order to encompass the range of exegetical studies available.

The method is an extension of form criticism. Whereas form criticism concerns itself with the structure and genre of particular texts, this method focuses upon the evolutionary development of that text and how it may have assumed different meanings over the years, thus communicating different messages to people over many generations. This method assumes that all literature evolves over time, especially if it is transmitted in oral form. So the entire sweep of a literary piece comes under consideration from its earliest oral form to its final position as a written text in the canon. This evolutionary trajectory is hypothesized about by the scholar through both oral and written stages of development, and such hypothesizing is a very subjective endeavor. In addition, this method is interested in how a text relates to passages around it—how cycles of texts grew into larger cycles of literature in the process of oral and written transmission. In that process of relating to those additional texts, a passage would take on additional meanings, perhaps even reversing its message depending on how the later editors crafted the growing collection of texts. The social and religious needs of people can be hypothesized about also in this process of growth. In many ways, a traditio-historical analysis combines both source criticism and form criticism in a sophisticated fashion. Perhaps one might call it a three-dimensional approach. It differs from source criticism by stressing the significance of oral transmission; it differs from form criticism by considering the evolution of the wider context in which a passage is found.

The method began with scholars who sought to move beyond those earlier critical methods, and early contributors, including Hermann Gunkel (1862–1932), Hugo Gressmann (1877–1927), August Klostermann (1837–1915), Albrecht Alt (1883–1956), and others, who sought to reconstruct the theoretical oral prehistory and original oral form of a literary biblical text. The later traditio-historical critics, many of whom were form critics already, Gerhard von Rad (1901–1971), Martin Noth (1902–1968), and Ivan Engnell (1906–1964), extended their evaluation to include a hypothetical consideration of all the stages of development for a biblical text from its original oral form to the final written text.

The object of their consideration included texts in the Pentateuch and the historical books (Joshua, Judges, Samuel, Kings) known as the Deuteronomistic History. Von Rad's seminal work suggested that the Pentateuch evolved out of short oral creeds, and that the Yahwist was the first tradition to combine the Sinai traditions with the accounts of the wilderness wanderings and conquest (von Rad). Noth advanced the theory that great cycles of oral tradition (patriarchs, exodus, wilderness, Sinai, and entrance into arable land) and some shorter cycles evolved into the Pentateuchal sources (the Yahwist, the Elohist, and the Priestly source), and that the Deuteronomistic History was composed by one creative author, not out of Pentateuchal sources, but out of diverse and fragmentary traditions (Noth 1972; 1981). Scandinavian scholars (also referred to loosely as the Uppsala School) contributed greatly to this method. They rejected literary or source criticism, saying the development of biblical traditions occurred primarily in the oral stage until precipitation into writing during the Babylonian exile, and hence the method was concerned only with oral tradition. Henrik Samuel Nyberg (1889–1974) may have begun the movement with a study of oral tradition in Hosea. Truly significant scholars included Ivan Engnell, who wrote numerous essays in critical methodology (Engnell) and Sigmund Mowinckel (1884–1965), who moderated between the Scandinavian emphasis on oral tradition and German source criticism (Mowinckel).

Exegetical analysis will differ for narratives, legal texts, prophetic oracles, psalms, wisdom sayings, novellas, and so forth. Certain texts lend themselves to a detailed traditio-historical scrutiny, especially if they appear to have a long evolutionary prehistory, as might be the case with narrative passages. In assessing a particular passage the critical scholar might envision various stages of development worthy of consideration, and depending upon the text, the critic may focus on one or more of these stages with intensity. The traditio-historical critic traces a text's development from its early oral formulation to its final literary form. At the first stage, the critic perceives it as an independent unit in a manner we would recognize as a form-critical assessment. The critic seeks to discover what ideas lie behind the formulation of the text, including possible parallels in contemporary ancient Near Eastern literature and conceptualizations. The critic considers other texts in the Old Testament that might have influenced the formulation of the passage, as well as other texts that might have been influenced by this passage. The greater social milieu of all the comparable texts may be discussed.

It must be admitted that not every biblical passage passed through a significant oral stage of transmission, but scholars generally assume that Pentateuchal and Deuteronomistic narratives as well as prophetic oracles and some psalms had an oral prehistory. Careful scrutiny of our present literary text may lead one to discern some of the stages of this developmental process, including the original form, message, and social setting. Thus, the traditio-historical critic seeks to answer several questions:

1. What was the original extent of the oral form in contrast to the present written text? What lines have been added secondarily in the later oral and written transmission?

2. What was the shape of the original oral form? Is there a discernible outline or pattern? Does this pattern conform to a genre that would have been recognized by its audience, such as epic, hero-tale, legend, myth, chronicle, fable, or song (for the narratives) or as lament, parable, lawsuit, disputation, salvation oracle, or taunt (for prophetic oracles)?

3. What was the original message, and how might it be different from the messages the text communicated in later oral and written stages?

4. Who spoke the original oral form (priests, Levites, bards, prophets), and why did this form originate with them?

5. To whom was the oral form addressed, and what were their needs to which this form spoke?

This analysis is form criticism, and for the traditio-historical critic it is now one stage in the process of exegesis.

Next, the critic seeks to trace the evolution of the passage in oral and written form, both in terms of the internal development of the passage (as in form criticism) and in terms of the passage's relation to the surrounding literary context (as in source criticism). In its evolutionary trajectory the text may have gone from being a loose oral account to becoming part of a larger oral or written source, such as the Yahwist or Elohist. Then as that "source" became synthesized with other accounts, our current biblical text began to take shape. Thus, the scholar traces the hypothetical emergence of a text in a growing cycle of literature whose process of growth stops only with the creation of a sacred canon (at which point canonical criticism takes over).

Once the oral narrative became part of a larger cycle, it func-
tioned in a larger theological tradition with overarching themes
that united a number of texts. The individual narrative became subordinate to the themes of the greater cycle, and whoever crafted the
larger oral or written corpus often changed some of the language in
the shorter forms to conform to these greater themes. The scholar
observes how the original text now relates to passages around it and
seeks to discover which of those passages might have been woven
together in a separate oral or written cycle at some point in transmission. Diverse texts are associated with each other on the basis
of common vocabulary, themes, and theological ideas. They are
distinguished from other passages which might have belonged to a
separate cycle of traditions because the latter are duplicate accounts
to those in the first cycle, or because the latter share their own common language over against the passages under consideration. Once
this distinct larger cycle of texts has been isolated, the critic seeks to
articulate its distinct theology or ideology.

At this stage the traditio-historical critic engages in what
traditionally has been called source or literary criticism. In Pentateuchal studies this would be the point where scholars evaluate
texts as being part of the Yahwist, Elohist, or Priestly tradition.
In the Deuteronomistic History scholars delineate cycles such as
the Rise of David (1 Sam 16—2 Sam 8), the Succession Narrative (2 Sam 9-20, 1 Kgs 1-2), or the Court History of Solomon
(1 Kgs 3-11). In legal corpora one would isolate the Book of the
Covenant (Exod 21-23), the Holiness Code (Lev 17-26), or the
Deuteronomic Laws (Deut 12-26). In the prophetic tradition one
would isolate early editions of each particular prophet's oracles,
which contain the core of the prophet's original oracles and early
additions by disciples.

Significant investigation envisions how the biblical text might
have grown into its present literary context. How did the passage
become connected with other texts, and how did that process
evolve through various stages? The traditio-historical critic is interested not only in the transformation of meaning experienced by
that passage as other texts are connected to it, but how the passage

fits into the greater cycle of texts in terms of meaning. (Early literary or source critics assumed this amalgamation of texts occurred in written fashion, but traditio-historical scholars assume these early collections or cycles might have arisen in oral form.)

How does the larger cycle of narratives connect to an even larger segment of literature? This occurs when the biblical texts most likely precipitated into written form. So the traditio-historical critic now asks how the original form and its larger cycle fit into a larger entity, such as the Deuteronomistic History (620–550 BCE), the Priestly edited version of the Pentateuchal narratives (550–400 BCE), the final written form of a prophetic book, such as Isaiah (with Proto-, Deutero-, and Trito-Isaiah brought together), or even the prophetic corpus as a whole. The critic inquires subjectively into how the even greater context affects the original passage, and how that passage adds to the message of the greater corpus.

The scholar is interested in an editorial process and observes additions to the text that appear literary and may be from scribal hands. These additions, as well as the way sources are woven together, reflect sophisticated theological assumptions, and clever literary style and intellectual depth is observable in the allusions, foreshadowings, genealogies, thematic speeches, editorial comments, and other literary links which unite large sections of literature. Early source critics often denigrated these later editorial additions, but in the past two generations we have come to respect these final editors as perhaps the most theologically profound contributors to the process.

The final area of reflection by the scholar is one in which traditio-historical critics too often have been remiss: the consideration of how the individual text fits into the message of the entire biblical canon. The scholar interested in this question reflects on how the original text(s) under consideration might have been used and reinterpreted by the later biblical tradition—such as within the books in the Ketuvim (Writings), generated in the postexilic era, or by authors of the New Testament. The critic wishes to discuss how the individual text fits into the message of the greater biblical canon and biblical theology as a whole.

This last level of reflection has been called canonical criticism by scholars who have advocated it in the last generation, including Brevard S. Childs (Childs 1970, 1974) and James A. Sanders (Sanders 1972, 2005). Though sometimes described as though it were a methodology separate from the other critical methods discussed above, canonical criticism is actually the final and theologically culminating stage of the traditio-historical method. At this point the exegete attempts to discern the religious message of the biblical text for people today.

The exegete might evaluate 1 Sam 3:1–21. It appears to be a complete story created in the form of a prophetic call narrative (according to some scholars) combined with an ancient Near Eastern (Mesopotamian) auditory message dream (in my opinion). At some point, the text became part of the Samuel Idyll in 1 Sam 1–3. At a later juncture, this material was combined with other short cycles to create the Rise of the Monarchy cycle in 1 Sam 1–15, which in turn became part of the books of Samuel and the greater Deuteronomistic History (Joshua through 2 Kings). Throughout this process, the text took on different shades of meaning in relation to the whole corpus of material. As the text became part of an increasingly larger corpus of oral or written literature, additional editorial statements were included, and the critic attempts to isolate those and suggest at what stage they were added. For example, 1 Sam 3:19–21 may have been added piecemeal in the later stages as the entire Deuteronomistic History emerged.

Goal of the Method

As the name implies, this method is a study of the "historical" development of the traditions and seeks to discover the message of the biblical passage. It is not history writing as some have mistakenly supposed, especially advocates of new forms of literary criticism, for we cannot easily reconstruct Israel's political or social history after tracing the steps of literary evolution (we might occasionally obtain a few insights, however). In reality, this method undertakes theological quests. It seeks to discover the ideational or theological messages of a text and its greater context as the literature grew and precipitated from oral to written form.

The theologian or preacher may derive many levels of meaning from a text, each representing what that text said to a particular community of belief. This can be a more rewarding technique than one that simply seeks a literal, spiritual, and allegorical interpretation of the text, as Christians undertook in the Middle Ages and early modern era, for that technique read the text in a rather flat fashion and overlooked any input concerning the social background of a text. This new method is a literary and theological "traditions development" evaluation, which seeks to unlock the many different meanings.

In retrospect, tradition history or the traditio-historical method evaluates the theoretic evolution of a biblical passage, and in so doing it absorbs the techniques of several other methods. It seeks to understand the message of a text at each stage of its evolution so to demonstrate the dynamic growth of the biblical tradition, as each generation reinterprets and develops its past traditions.

Theological Significance

The importance of the method is found in its ability, not only to attempt a reconstruction of the oral and literary evolution of biblical texts, but to discern the meaning of the message at each stage of development. Above all, the method implies that the biblical text is not a static repository of absolute truths revealed by God, but the record of a dynamic process of human and divine interaction over many generations, in which sacred texts are received and then reinterpreted by subsequent generations. My assertion may imply that the tradition-making process is part of revelation itself (Knight). It further implies that sacred texts may contain several levels of meaning, as those meanings have been imparted by successive generations of transmitters—the sacred texts are polyvalent, capable of multiple interpretations even today. Consequently, from the texts the modern reader may draw upon a wealth of meaning, which lies beneath a surface reading and may be suggested creatively by the critical scholar for use in contemporary theology, pedagogy, preaching, and piety.

Critics, especially advocates of structuralism and new literary-critical methods, have assailed the method for being too historically minded—that is, attempting to reconstruct the history of Israel from the very subjective analysis of literary texts. Much of this criticism is deserved, for too often biblical scholars attempted to reconstruct history. The history of Israel may be reconstructed only with a subtle interplay of archaeological data, critical analysis of literary texts, and application of appropriate social-scientific and anthropological models. The traditio-historical method, as well as the other methods (source, form, redaction, and so forth), are not historical in the sense that a historian would recognize. Rather, they seek to trace ideational and religious development in a sacred text and to perceive its growth in relationship to other texts in the canon. Observations concerning social settings are really incidental, though helpful, and obviously quite subjective. To think that this method can reconstruct the history of Israel is to misunderstand the nature of the historical quest.

In general, the tradition history method should be seen as primarily a subjective and creative art, not an empirical, scientific method. This critical methodology is scientific only in that it rigorously analyzes a text, sets aside theological and denominational beliefs, the assumptions of modern interpreters, and temporarily suspends the meaning imparted to a particular text by the rest of the biblical tradition. Also, the method may be scientific in that occasionally, historical, archaeological, and social-scientific data may facilitate understanding the biblical passage under scrutiny. The method attempts to be "scientific" only in that the interpreter tries to be rigorously objective. Yet ultimately the reconstruction of the prior evolutionary development of a literary text is a subjective and hypothetical task. This is evidenced by the multitude of diverse interpretations rendered by scholars on any given biblical text. In the face of such interpretive incertitude should we disparage the method? No! The purpose of the method is not to ascertain ultimate truth or the perfect reconstruction of a process which can no longer be empirically observed. Rather, the method is suggestive and creative—it offers possibilities for understanding meanings which lie latent in the biblical text. The scholar humbly offers new possibilities for understanding texts to the reader, the theologian, the preacher, the student, and the person of faith, in order to enhance their insight and appreciation of the Bible.

Biblical Examples of Traditio-Historical Criticism

Two examples are given of the method here. The first observes the hypothetical evolution of two related biblical texts: the Decalogues in Exod 20 and Deut 5. This example summarizes part of my article "Deuteronomic Redaction and the Evolution of the Decalogues in Exodus 20 and Deuteronomy 5," *International Journal of Research in Humanities and Social Studies* 11.2 (2024) 19–29. The second example observes how a text evolves in its relationship to other texts: 1 Sam 3. It is drawn from my essay "Tradition History" in *Dictionary of Biblical Interpretation*, 2 vols., edited by John Hayes (Nashville: Abingdon, 2004), 2:583–88.

Exodus 20 and Deuteronomy 5

In this representative traditio-historical analysis, I will work backwards, going from the final form of two texts to the theoretical original shorter form. Not all critical scholars would agree that the two Decalogues went through this evolution; they would maintain that the two codes arose late and were inspired piecemeal by other law codes. Nevertheless, I have always sensed that the two codes lend themselves quite well to a hypothetical evolutionary trajectory which can be reconstructed by carefully considering the final forms of both codes.

At the first stage of our analysis, we should isolate what is unique to each of the Decalogues in Exod 20 and Deut 5. We could then assume that those unique portions were added to each

Decalogue by its respective editors at a late stage in the evolutionary process.

What appears to be distinctive for the Decalogues in Exod 20 and Deut 5 are the following items:

First, the verb in Exod 20 in the command regarding the Sabbath is "remember" or *ZKR*. The word has cultic or memorial festival connotations. Believers are to "remember" the great acts of God in saving people, or they are to "remember" the Passover, which means to celebrate it. Thus, this is a word which has cultic or priestly connotations. The word in Deut 5 by comparison is *SHMR*, which means "to keep" or "obey." That word has much more of the nuance of the commands found elsewhere in Deuteronomy, which are more civil in nature. It is possible that an older form of the Decalogue used neither verb.

Second, both Sabbath commands find it necessary to list explicitly the people who should not work on the Sabbath. One gets the impression that this list grew over the years to communicate clearly who should be given rest because everyone from simple farmers to large slave owning agriculturalists sought to get work out of someone on the Sabbath. One could envision a slave owner being told that his slave could not work, so then the slave owner would declare that the animal which pulled the plow did the work and not the slave who walked behind the animal and the plow. Lawgivers found it necessary to list even animals along with people as blessed by the Sabbath rest.

When we compare the two codes, we discover that Deut 5:14 found it necessary to specifically add "ox" and "donkey" along with the word for "livestock," found in both codes. Perhaps, because the word for "livestock" could also more narrowly mean "cattle," someone could declare that an ox or a donkey could pull the plow since they were not cattle. Hence, the author of Deut 5 felt obligated to specifically mention the "ox" and the "donkey" prior to the phrase "or any of your livestock." The editors of the Deut 5 text seem to have been more concerned with working out such logical details.

Deut 5:14 also adds specifically "your male and female slave should rest as you do." This is because Deuteronomy elsewhere provides special protection for slaves, and so an additional plea for slaves' rights is included here. Furthermore, this little phrase leads into a longer section which is unique to Deuteronomy. The editors of the Exod 20 text may not have been concerned with such issues.

Third, at this point the texts in Exod 20 and Deut 5 significantly part ways. Exod 20:11 connects the observation of the Sabbath to the creation of the world. In an obvious reference to Gen 1, the editor of Exod 20 declares that because God rested on the seventh day of creation and blessed that day, so we must observe it. The Priestly origin of Gen 1 increases our suspicion that the final editor of Exod 20 is also of Priestly origin. By way of contrast, the final editor of Deut 5 appeals to the exodus event and the liberation of slaves from Egypt as a rationale for Sabbath observance (Deut 5:15). Though the texts do not declare this clearly, one gets the impression that the Exod 20 version primarily views the Sabbath as a holy day and perhaps a day of worship, whereas the stress in Deut 5 is on the Sabbath as a day of rest for slaves and free people alike. The emphasis upon worship reflects Priestly concerns, and the emphasis upon physical rest may reflect prophetic concerns with justice for all people and especially rights for the poor and enslaved. Though both Decalogue versions convey that the exodus from Egypt is a fundamental theological concern in Israel, we are unable to discern from how each version interprets the exodus event, which version is older.

Fourth, though they are minor details, Deuteronomy added extra language to the commands on Sabbath and obedience to parents. After the initial command, Deut 5:12 and Deut 5:16 both add, "as the LORD your God has commanded you." These phrases appear to be a reference to an earlier law, perhaps even the Decalogue in Exodus (Nielsen 37–38). Why the reference would appear in these two commands and not at the beginning of the Decalogue in Deut 5, however, is puzzling. Furthermore, Deut 5:16 adds, "that it may go well with you" after the blessing of a long life and before the reference to how Yahweh is giving the land to the people. The author thus adds "prosperity" to "long life" as a blessing for obedience to this command. The idea of prosperity in the land resulting from obedience to God is a typical motif in Deuteronomy (Deut 4:40; 5:26; 6:3, 18; 12:25, 28; 22:27) (Nielsen 41–42).

Fifth, in the command against false witness Exod 20:16 uses *SHQR* for "false" and Deut 5:20 uses *SHWA* for "false." *SHWA* is also used in Exod 20:7 and Deut 5:11 in conjunction with the command on misuse of the LORD's name. Perhaps *SHQR* was the original verb, and in Deut 5:20 *SHWA* displaces *SHQR* simply because it was used with the earlier command on the name. This might be attributed to Deuteronomic editors, but no good reason can be given for the change.

Sixth, the next truly significant difference occurs with the coveting commands. In Exodus the imperative not to covet the neighbor's house comes before the command not to covet the neighbor's wife, and Deuteronomy reverses them. Perhaps the original form of the Decalogue placed house first, because the term also means "family," and the wife is part of the family. In the early days of Israel's history when most people owned little property other than their essentials for life, the term for "house" would have been understood primarily as "family." In later years with the rise of wealth and an affluent class of people, the term *house* could refer to accumulated wealth in the minds of many. In such an age it would be necessary for the word "wife" to be placed before "house" in order to ensure that women not be perceived as part of the house or as property of the men, or least that they not be seen as less important than physical property (if the two commands are to be seen as distinctly separate). It would occur to a reform-oriented prophetic editor to transpose these two imperatives; hence, the switch is found in Deuteronomy, a book which elsewhere shows great concern for the rights of women. Such a transposition would not be of great concern for Priestly editors, however, who may retain the sequence handed down to them in an older version of the Decalogue.

Seventh, Deut 5:21 adds "field" after the term *house* as something not to be desired. This, too, may indicate Deuteronomy's awareness of a more advanced economic situation in which land is a significant commodity owned by people. By pairing "field" with "house," the imperative makes "house" even more clearly refer to physical property, thus necessitating the placement of "wife" before "house."

Eighth, a small but interesting observation is the use of a different verb for one of the "covet" imperatives in Deut 5:21. Whereas Exod 20 uses the verb *HMD*, which means "to seize, desire, or take plans to get," Deut 5:21 uses the verb *AWH* for "covet," and it has more of the meaning of psychological desire. The first verb, *HMD*, is more concrete and may denote human activity such as fraud or extortion, which was punishable in a court of law; the second verb, *AWH*, denotes an inner mental activity not punishable by law. The second verb denotes the kind of mental activity that we have come to connect with this commandment. Those who believe that the Decalogue evolved from being a civil law code, in which the violation of the commands might have warranted the death penalty in some or all instances, into a moral code may point to this subtle transformation from a verb of physical activity (*HMD*) into a verb denoting an interior mental disposition (*AWH*). If correct, this perception would be a significant sign of the process of evolution connected with the Decalogue. Deut 5 here reflects some later developments in the interpretation of the Decalogue for everyday life.

Once we have eliminated the portions of the text that are distinct in Exod 20 and Deut 5, we can look at what remains and perhaps assume that there was a prior edition of the Decalogue inherited by both the Priestly editors of Exod 20 and the prophetic editors of Deuteronomy 5.

Yet now a different perspective presents itself. As we survey both Exod 20 and Deut 5, we find language in both texts that sounds very Deuteronomic. This material could be removed without affecting the basic message of the commands. What if it, too, was at some point added to an even older version of the Decalogue?

The so-called prophetic editors of Deut 5 have used Deuteronomic language. What if we were to assume either that Deuteronomic-prophetic editors added common material to both Exod 20 and Deut 5, or—better said—that an editor added this material to the Decalogue before it split into the two versions that have come to us? We could envision two possible scenarios: (1) A Deuteronomic theologian edits the Decalogue, which is subsequently inherited by a later Priestly and later prophetic editors. (2) Deuteronomic editors transform the text in both Exod 20 and Deut 5. Then, later Priestly editors transform Exod 20 and change the text back into a simpler form. By this I mean the Priestly editors removed the reference to "ox and donkey" in 5:14 and the reference to property in 5:16, placed "house" before "wife" in 5:21, and removed the verb form "desire" in the same verse. I doubt this is a likely scenario. Hence, I prefer the first option. I suggest that a prior Deuteronomic editor was a *traditur* in the transmission of the Decalogue before it was received by the Priestly editors of Exod 20 and the prophetic editors of Deut 5.

If such an editor existed, what textual materials did this person insert? The choice of such passage is somewhat selective, but they might include the following:

Exod 20:2/Deut 5:6: "who brought you out of the land of Egypt, out of the house of slavery."

Exod 20:4/Deut 5:8: "whether in the form of anything that is in the heaven above, or that is on the earth beneath, or that is in the water under the earth."

Exod 20:5–6/Deut 5:9–10: "You shall not bow down to them or worship them; for I the LORD your God am a jealous God, punishing children for the iniquity of parents, to the third and fourth generation of those who reject me, but showing steadfast love to the thousandth generation of those who love me and keep my commandments."

Exod 20:7/Deut 5:11: "for the LORD will not acquit anyone who misuses his name."

Exod 20:9–10/Deut 5:13–14: "Six days you may labor and do all your work. But the seventh day is a sabbath to the LORD your God; you shall not do any work—you, your son or your daughter, your male or female slave, your livestock, or the alien resident in your towns."

Exod 20:12/Deut 5:16: "so that your days may be long in the land that the LORD your God is giving to you."

Exod 20:17/Deut 5:21: "or your male or female slave, or ox, or donkey, or anything that belongs to your neighbor."

Once these materials have been eliminated, what remains appears to be a basic Decalogue. It is very similar to the commandments we memorized as children. But even at this point we could theoretically eliminate words that have the appearance of being added in the early years of oral transmission for the sake of clarification. To isolate such words, of course, is very subjective, but if we were to hypothetically do this, the following might be words to be eliminated.

v. 2: "your God" simply clarifies who the LORD is.

v. 3: "besides me" is superfluous to the essential commandment.

v. 4: "for yourselves" might be superfluous.

v. 7: "of the LORD" need not be mentioned, since it is obvious from the first command that LORD is the name of the deity.

v. 8: "to keep holy" need not be mentioned, since the verb "remember" (ZKR) or "observe" (SHMR) is sufficient.

v. 12: perhaps "and your mother" was added, or perhaps another word stood in the place of "father and mother," such as the word "old ones" or "elders" (ZQNM).

v. 16: "against your neighbor" is superfluous to the command.

At this point we could stop, for we have hypothetically reconstructed a short form of the commandments. This is a form that feasibly could have been carved into tablets of stone. Even if such carving never occurred, the commandments should have been in shortened form at some point in the transmission to give rise to the tradition that Moses did carve them on tablets of stone. Thus, the commands may have conformed to a fiction.

Subsequent reconstruction of the commandments is extremely hypothetical, and some scholars are very reluctant to change words in the text so drastically. Nevertheless, here are some of the suggestions:

First, perhaps all the commandments were originally stated in negative form. Since the verbs are different in the Deut 5 and Exod 20 versions of the Sabbath command, it does not seem too radical to suggest that yet a different verb altogether may have originally been used. Perhaps the original command was "do not dishonor the Sabbath" (Nielsen 103). Once "dishonor" was removed, it is then understandable why two different verbs, "remember" and "observe," arose to replace it. "Dishonor" (*KLL*) may have been removed because it is a strong verb that can also mean "blaspheme" or "curse," and such a strong word should not appear in texts proximate to the divine name. This verb is placed in the margins in other parts of the Hebrew Bible, and the verb "bless" (*BRK*) takes its place in the actual text, thus indicating discomfort with the appearance of the word *KLL* in sacred texts or with its proximity to the divine name. Likewise, the parental command might have originally been, "do not dishonor your father," or if we emend the text even more, we might read, "Do not dishonor your elders." This would explain why the later meanings of the command would have evolved into respect for parents and respect for those in authority. "Elders" would contain the nuance of both parents and leaders of the community. There is also the issue of the two different words used in the command against bearing false witness: *SHQR* in Exod 20:16 and *SHWA* in Deut 5:20. As mentioned above, it may be that *SHKR* was the original word, but *SHWA* replaced it in Deut 5:20.

Second, the other issue is the number of the commands. In addition to the expression, "I am the LORD," there are twelve commandments, if one wishes to count the imperative "Do no bow down before them" in conjunction with the prohibition of images. Jews and Christians over the years, however, believe that particular imperative simply is an elaboration upon the imperative not to make idols. We likewise have treated it as a Deuteronomic addition. That, however, leaves us with "I am the LORD" and eleven imperatives. The expression "I am the LORD" appears in legal sequences in the book of Leviticus (Lev 18:5; 19:2) and must be counted as a command to give these sequences a numerical total of either ten or twelve imperatives. Therefore, many (including traditional Jews) count "I am the LORD" as a command. If this is the case, then originally the Ten Commandments would have been the Twelve Commandments. There are several advantages to this enumeration theory. We no longer have to combine two of the commands: Roman Catholics and Lutherans combine "no other gods" and "no images," following the opinion of Augustine around 400 CE. Protestants in general combine the two coveting commands, and orthodox Jews combine both sets, since "I am the LORD" is the first command for them. The second advantage is that Exod 20 corresponds more closely to the twelve commands in the Decalogue in Exod 34 (if we are counting the commands correctly there). According to our Exodus narrative, Exod 34 is the second giving of the Decalogue to Moses. Actually, these two separate codes may have been parallel codes, one civil (Exod 20) and one ritual (Exod 34) for Israelites in the early years. The narrative clearly presents both. It would make sense if both codes had twelve commands. The problem with this reconstruction is that Exod 34:28 refers to the commands in Exod 20 as the ten words, which implies we should count them as ten commands in Exod 20. Perhaps that expression referred to something else that has been dropped from the narrative (an extremely hypothetical suggestion). We do not know. Thus, our hypothetical reconstruction of the "Twelve Commandments" must remain only an interesting hypothesis.

1 Samuel 3

Let us consider another text for analysis by the traditio-historical method, 1 Sam 3, in order to see how it evolves with the stories that surround it (Gnuse 1984). The five stages of evaluation for the critical scholar would be as follows:

(1) A review of ancient Near Eastern literature would focus upon comparable prophetic narratives and dream reports. Mesopotamian sources offer many suggestive parallels, especially nighttime prophetic dream reports received in shrines at Mari (1800 BCE).

Even more relevant are dream reports from Egypt and Mesopotamia, which fall into patterns of "auditory message dreams" and "visual symbolic dreams." Comparison of these findings with 1 Sam 3 demonstrates striking similarities with "auditory message dreams."

(2) Form-critical evaluation of 1 Sam 3:1–21 leads scholars to sense that the original form of the text was vv. 1–18. In the plot development of the narrative there are sensitive literary devices, including the artistic contrast of innocent young Samuel and the old priest Eli, who had failed to control his evil sons, and the three-fold call of Samuel by Yahweh designed to heighten the suspense of an impending theophany in an age when the "word of the LORD" was rare. At this point the scholar observes form-critical similarities between this text and other biblical prophetic call narratives (Moses, Exod 3; Gideon, Judg 6; Saul, 1 Sam 9; Jeremiah, Jer 1; and Ezekiel, Ezek 1–2), as well as the auditory message dreams of Assyria and Chaldean Babylon (700–550 BCE). The account appears crafted to conform to both formats.

(3) The scholar then observes how 1 Sam 3 fits into the greater Samuel Idyll in 1 Sam 1–3, which as a whole contrasts the young prophet with the evil priests. This cycle shares themes with the larger cycle called the Elohist in the Pentateuch, which likewise has auditory message dreams in the patriarchal accounts, a positive attitude toward prophets, and a distrust of priests (Exod 32–33, the Golden Calf incident). How the Samuel Idyll is connected to the Elohist tradition is highly debated, however.

(4) The critical scholar expands the observation of how 1 Sam 3 fits into its greater context by observing further redaction. First Sam 1–3 became part of the narrative cycle concerning the rise of the monarchy in 1 Sam 1–15, wherein old narratives sympathetic to the monarchy (1 Sam 9:1—10:16, 11, 13–14) appear woven together with later (perhaps Deuteronomistic) texts critical of kingship (1 Sam 7–8, 10:17–27, 12, 15). The Samuel Idyll reinforces a pejorative perception of Saul and kingship by stressing the sufficiency of Samuel as Israel's leader, and the general superiority of prophets over kings. This editorial work appears to come from Deuteronomistic Historians. The same editors then connected

1 Sam 1–15 with other major sections of literature to create the books of 1 and 2 Samuel, wherein the decline of Saul before David is justified, and David becomes a standard by which to evaluate other kings in the history of 1 and 2 Kings. First Sam 3 plays a pivotal rule in preparing for the unfolding of later history and stressing the prophetic word as an ultimate authority.

(5) On a canonical level the critic may observe how the Deuteronomistic History fits into the greater biblical theological message of the Old Testament, especially in regard to themes such as covenant, obedience, divine revelation, and prophetic calling. 1 Sam 3 contributes to all these themes. Canonical criticism also draws the traditio-historical critic into reflection upon how 1 Sam 3 foreshadows Jesus in the infancy narratives of Matt 1–2 (where auditory message dreams occur again) and Luke 1–2. The prophet Samuel foreshadows the prophetic ministry of Jesus, who also opposed corrupt priests. Hence, 1 Sam 3 ultimately unites with other texts that proclaim the nature of the prophetic calling which all Jews and Christians seek to heed.

In conclusion the traditio-historical critical method is a very full and well-developed method. It absorbs the source-critical and form-critical function in tracing the evolutionary trajectory of a biblical passage, and in its final stage it should engage in canonical criticism. Throughout this process it asks what the passage's message is at each stage of its development. Thus, I am tempted to suggest that this method lends itself to the theological task more than other methods.

5

NEW CRITICAL APPROACHES

CRITICAL APPROACHES TO ANALYZING biblical texts have emerged in the last sixty years, which have often been characterized by their advocates as new ultimate critical methodologies. I would prefer to think of them not as critical methodologies for interpreting biblical texts, but rather as approaches to the biblical texts that can be combined with other critical methodologies to provide a fuller understanding of any given text. Canonical criticism, which seeks to interpret a biblical passage in light of the entire biblical canon, is the last step in a truly thorough traditio-historical analysis. Social-scientific analysis is an intensive investigation of the sociological and cultural background of a passage, which likewise can dovetail nicely with any of the interpretative methodologies. Thus, I use the term *approaches* rather than "methodologies" to describe these interpretative styles or techniques.

Canonical Criticism

This approach will forever be connected to Brevard S. Childs (1923–2007), who called for this use of a method that evaluated the meaning of a biblical text in the light of the entire canon. He called for this approach (Childs 1970) and then sought to demonstrate its function in his commentary on the book of Exodus in the Old Testament Library commentary series (Childs 1974). Childs believed that the only way to truly understand a biblical text was to see it in the total light of the rest of Scripture or the canon, since the book was indeed placed into a collection of writings. Only with a consideration of the text's relationship to the rest of the canon can the text be properly interpreted for the believing community. However, the actual term *canonical criticism* was coined by James A. Sanders (1927–2020) in his 1972 book, *Torah and Canon* (Sanders 1972, 2005). Childs subsequently did not like the term *canonical criticism*, for he did not see this approach as a critical method for analyzing texts, but rather it was more of a hermeneutical approach. I would agree with him.

There were two dimensions for this process of interpretation, as Childs so aptly demonstrated in his commentary on Exodus. The passage under consideration had to be understood in relationship to the rest of the biblical text. In this regard, the methodology looked to be the last stage of a traditio-historical process of interpretation wherein the focus was on how the text is brought together with the other texts to create a biblical book. But Childs also included a study of how the biblical passage under consideration would continue to be interpreted in light of the later Jewish and Christian interpretations for their respective believing communities. This methodology was particularly interested in the books of the Torah or Pentateuch. As critics noted, such an evaluation that included the history of interpretation for a passage would create a massive commentary. So many things are said by church fathers, and the multitude of things that are said about biblical passages by Protestant Reformers are intimidating. (I would not wish to undertake this task for the book of Genesis!)

But Childs and others have a good point. Any biblical text has ultimately become part of the canon. If you are a faithful traditio-historical critic who seeks to explicate how an individual passage becomes part of an increasingly larger and larger corpus of literature, you finally must say something about its relationship to the entire Bible. Thus, to repeat: canonical criticism is the last stage of the traditio-historical method. Separating canonical criticism from the traditio-historical method results in, I believe, simply a "flat" reading of the text, which can float into a form of naïve literalism, and possibly a fundamentalism that gives birth to so many egregious misunderstandings of the Bible. The good canonical critic is a person deeply rooted in the other critical methodologies.

Social-Scientific Criticism

The advocates of this method speak of it as though it were a new critical methodology. However, one might argue that it is a way of analyzing texts with comparative materials rather than a methodology. The chief advocates for this approach to biblical texts include Bruce J. Malina (1933–2017) and John J. Pilch (1936–2016). Their venue for publication was most often *Biblical Theology Bulletin*. Most of their contributions were in the field of New Testament studies. Their argument was that a study of the ancient world with its social values, social relations, group functions, rituals, and social view of reality could significantly increase our understanding of biblical texts. This approach appears to me to be a significant expansion of the traditio-historical methodology in its emphasis upon the social and historical background of the biblical texts.

The approach appears to be most productive when applied to narratives in the Gospels or to an assessment of Paul's urban audience. It plumbs the depths of how early listeners to the gospels or to epistles of Paul would have perceived what was being said differently than we do today because their social and cultural experiences were so different from ours in the modern age. In the Gospels an overriding concern is purity, and we do not sense that resonating in the accounts as would they. Additionally, east Mediterranean honor was an emotional and personal agenda in the narratives that transcends our comparable feelings. Social scientists have especially brought new light and new life to Gospel texts (especially healing accounts). The method can produce significant new insights in the consideration of specific texts.

In the Old Testament, however, the method does not approach individual accounts as effectively as in the New Testament.

Social-scientific criticism often dovetails with study of economic and historical concerns in assessing larger segments of literature. The social scientist will be concerned with the identity of the Israelites as pastoralists or as members of a dimorphic society that is both pastoral and agricultural. The finest work in this respect is *The Tribes of Yahweh* (1979), by Norman K. Gottwald (1926–2022). Consider also his general introduction to the Old Testament (Gottwald 1985) and some of his collected essays (2016, 2017, 2018). His assessment addresses the entire settlement process (or revolutionary process, in his opinion) operative in ancient Israel that created the entity of Israel in the highlands of Palestine. Other significant social-scientific assessments likewise addressed broader issues. Carol Meyers (1942–) evaluated women's roles in Israelite households in two significant works (Meyers 2005, 2012). D. N. Prenmath (1950–) provided a detailed study on the political, economic, and social background of the prophetic movement of the eighth century BCE using archaeological evidence (Premnath 2003). Marvin L. Chaney (1936–) brought together a collection of papers and essays addressing similar issues throughout Israel's history (Chaney 2017). An excellent collection of essays was edited by Philip F. Esler, *Ancient Israel: The Old Testament in Its Social Context*, 2006), which covers a wide range of Old Testament topics, key concepts, and biblical books. entire prophetic movement, or genealogies in general. Overall, the social-scientific method in the Old Testament focuses not so much on individual texts, as in New Testament studies, but upon significant aspects of life and culture of ancient Israel.

The chief problem of the method is that if you try to define this approach in detailed fashion and discuss scholars who are its advocates, you realize how broad and diffuse the method is, and it appears to have no boundaries. In a sense, this is a method that seeks to discuss the historical and social background to biblical texts. That is not a critical method, but it is simply research doing the groundwork for the discussion of any biblical text. You could begin to list many scholars in the nineteenth and twentieth centuries who did this form of commentary when they spoke of the historical, social, economic, and cultural background of ancient Israel. It would be unrealistic to attempt listing scholars who fall into this category.

If you attempt to be more concrete in defining the method, you will select those scholars who use the models of a particular sociologist or political thinker. Those scholars often define themselves as "social scientists," and they describe their approach as "social-scientific." (Commentators in the more numerous first group might be quick to disown the characterization of being "social scientists.") These scholars, who may specialize in a particular social-scientific model, might be especially attracted to the writings of Max Weber (1864–1920) (a sociologist who wrote a work on ancient Judaism) or Karl Marx (1818–1883) (a philosopher and early political scientist). Norman Gottwald's aforementioned work most certainly is indebted to Marx. Again, the parameters of the social-scientific model can become somewhat vague with this second group of scholars, for there are a host of sociologists and political thinkers on whom biblical commentators can be dependent. I thought of myself as being rooted in the thought of Eric Vogelin (1901–1985), but I would never have considered myself a social-scientific critic of biblical texts. So when the discussion becomes detailed, social-scientific criticism becomes rather vague. Only a few people in New Testament scholarship appear to really comfortably fit into the paradigm of social-scientific critics.

6

STRUCTURALISM

THIS METHOD APPEARED AND was hailed by its advocates as the critical approach to the Bible that would transcend and ultimately replace the historical-critical methods in general. It was praised as superior because it did not merely attempt to reconstruct history, but it plumbed the depths of meaning in the biblical texts. (I was in graduate school with a number of structuralists in the 1970s. They were nice people, enthusiastic cheerleaders for their method.) This methodology seeks the deep psychological structures within the text, purporting to discover meaning that mere historical criticism cannot obtain. Structuralists seek to interpret the text as a whole, and not break it into parts in some traditio-historical analysis. They do, however, seek to analyze component parts from a psychological-literary perspective.

Structuralism uses semiotics or linguistic theories to discern how meaningful communications occur through language and the grammar of sentences. It attempts to understand all means of human communication through discourses both orally and in written texts in order to discover how meaning is produced and communicated. The term *structural* is used because its advocates seek to identify different features in a given text and to show how these features relate to each other in a coherent whole, or structure. The critic observes all that can be seen in a text, including the smallest features such as syllables and words up to the larger phenomena, sentences, paragraphs, metaphors, and symbolic allusions. Literary phenomena merit close attention: characters, actions, situations, plots, and subplots, for instance.

The method is inspired by folklorist Vladimir Propp (1895–1970), literary theorist Algirdas Julien Greimas (1917–1992), and semiologist Ferdinand de Saussure (1857–1913), who studied the structure of language. Roman Jakobson (1896–1982) coined the term *structuralism*, and Roland Barthes (1915–1980) and Michel Foucault (1924–1986) influenced the approach. It was used in a number of intellectual fields, not just biblical studies. Propp studied Russian folktales to determine their structural units; Greimas did work in literary theory and literary structure of discourse; Saussure was a linguist and philosopher, Jakobson was a linguist and literary theorist, Barthes was a literary theorist and philosopher, and Foucault was a philosopher and historian. As a result of their influence, the structuralism that has influenced biblical structuralists is linguistic, anthropological, and literary analysis.

In biblical studies it is difficult to define the movement in general because different biblical scholars who use the methodology do different things in their analysis of the biblical text. Essentially, by using semiotics and psychology combined with literary theory, they look for the underlying paradigms in a narrative that are not readily apparent. These are subconscious patterns communicated by archetypal images. They seek to discern the component parts or units that make up these underlying structures. Proponents perceive biblical narratives to be like myths, which seek to resolve tensions or the opposition of great realities in life, such as life and death. For example, for a structuralist the theme of hunting in a biblical narrative might seek to resolve the tension between killing an animal (death) and obtaining food for human sustenance (life). This is called mediation.

Structuralists are interested in the social and cultural background of biblical narratives because this helps them to understand the tensions that are in the mind of the author. Above all, structuralists believe that there are deep "structures" within a text that can be discovered or decoded using their methodology.

In their analysis of a text, one observes diagrams that trace the movement of the narrative or plot and also the movements of the actors in the story; such movement in turn reveals the psychological direction of the literary characters. The reader is led to understand what the characters are truly doing and hence perceives the narrative intent of the biblical author. A simple historical-critical reading will never find these realia, according to the structuralists, which makes their reading methodology vastly superior. Chief proponents include primarily New Testament scholars with a sprinkling of Old Testament scholars. Prominent among these scholars are Dan Via (1929–2014) and Daniel Patte (1939–2024) (Patte 1975).

Among Old Testament scholars, some authors stand out significantly, including Robert Polzin (1977; 1980; 1989; 1993) and David Jobling (1941–) (1978 [= 1986a], 1986b). Polzin (1937–), in particular, analyzed literature in a "synchronic literary" fashion. He appeared to engage in both literary criticism and structuralism. Polzin considered a larger corpus of texts rather than a single text, and observed how passages in a biblical book such as 1 Samuel or 2 Samuel refer and allude to each other so as to present a fuller psychological message about a character's actions and intentions. Such intertextual analysis more deeply plumbs the message of these texts as they reinforce significant meanings for listeners. Jobling does likewise, analyzing shorter segments of literature in the Bible in a reflective literary and psychological fashion and paying close attention to individual vocabulary.

Structuralism impresses me as a very sophisticated form criticism that involves using psychology in its analysis of the "form." One structuralist who became somewhat disenchanted with the method noted that you committed tremendous energy to studying folklore and semiotics in order to discover in biblical texts what you could already discern with form criticism. But structuralism is a very interesting approach to the biblical text that does at times yield significant insights. It appears to be most adept in analyzing narratives in the Gospels.

A Biblical Example of Structuralism

Most structuralism articles are written on New Testament texts, but an excellent example of the structuralist methodology on an Old Testament text is provided by James L. Crenshaw in his article, "Journey into Oblivion: A Structural Analysis of Gen. 22:1–19," *Soundings: An Interdisciplinary Journal* 58 (1975) 243–56.

Crenshaw describes in vivid fashion the "monstrous" commision by God to Abraham concerning the imperative to offer up Isaac as a human sacrifice. As the story unwinds, Crenshaw emphasizes the painful silence between Abraham and Isaac during their journey to the mountain, the dutiful attitude of Isaac, and the haunted psyche of Abraham over the impending murder of his only son. The two nameless lads who accompany Abraham and Isaac add to this dark feeling, for nothing is said of them except that they were there. Even after Isaac is saved by God's decision to have Abraham sacrifice a ram instead of his son, there is no hint of rejoicing. A somber and dark mood continues to hang over the narrative. The story is doleful, and one is left with the image of an unsavory deity who so plays with the heartstrings of his faithful patriarch and his son. Crenshaw describes this mood in masterful fashion.

The structuralist analysis is often interested in movement of the characters in the narrative, and it does not disappoint us here. Crenshaw observes that there are four literary characters in the account: two lads who accompany Abraham and then both Abraham and Isaac. The unnamed lads travel from the home of Abraham to the foot of the mountain, but not up the mountain. They do not see or recognize the drama that occurs. They then return home with Abraham after he rejoins them at the foot of the mountain. Abraham travels to the mountain and up to the top of the mountain, then he returns down the mountain and travels home. Isaac travels to the mountain, up the mountain, but the biblical text makes no mention of his returning down the mountain and home. What happened to Isaac? Did he get sacrificed after all? Did he stay on the mountain? No. But the structuralist senses that the biblical author is telling us something. Isaac is forever alienated from a father who would slay him. Symbolically he does remain on the mountain. Perhaps his heart will forever remain on that mountain. He will not go home as Abraham's son ever again. In fact, Isaac appears in Genesis narratives with Abraham after that horrible experience on the mountain only at his father's burial. The symbolic movements of the characters in the narrative tell us something that the actual words of the narrative do not. The message is poignant. Isaac does not "return" with Abraham. He has been "sacrificed."

Crenshaw displays this deep psychological message of the text by a classic structuralist diagram that uses all the symbols generated by structuralist critics (which I barely understand). It is a map of motion, but it is a map that comments upon the deeper psychological message of the story with the perception of that motion. The two lads return home, Abraham returns home, but Isaac disappears. It is a tragic account of faithfulness to God and father-son alienation. The structuralist analysis unveils it.

New Testament scholars find structuralist analysis most effective with the parables of Jesus and the movement of the characters in those parables. Old Testament scholars find the method effective especially with larger narrative segments.

7

NEW LITERARY CRITICISMS

SINCE 1960 A NUMBER of newer methodologies, influenced by scholarship in literature, have made significant inroads in biblical study. Generically called new literary criticism, these approaches try to appreciate the literary quality found in the final text as a unity. Hence, they often criticize the other higher critical methods for dissecting and overanalyzing the text. These new methods are interested in the beauty of the text without inquiring into the development or social-historical background. In a certain way, these methods arose out of form criticism and apply interdisciplinary techniques from the fields of literature and psychology. These methods bring to the field of biblical studies the skills and insights of literary scholars. These methods seek to evaluate and appreciate the literary value of the biblical text and to evaluate it as great art worthy of appreciation rather to probe its historical origins or the evolution of a particular text.

Rhetorical Criticism

By some of its early practitioners rhetorical criticism was also called *aesthetic criticism* and sometimes *structural criticism* (not to be confused with *structuralism*), which reflects, in part, what this approach to the biblical text seeks to accomplish. The method sidesteps the traditional critical approaches to the biblical text, which seek to reconstruct an original form of the narrative prior to our present written text. Practitioners appreciate the present form of the text and how it effectively communicates to an ancient or modern audience, especially with the artistic devices that give unity or meaning to the passage. Their concern would not be with the historical development or theological meaning, but rather with literary beauty and timeless existential meaning. Simply put, they appreciate the "rhetoric" of the text—both how it effectively communicated to its original audience and likewise how it speaks deftly to the modern audience. They study how the biblical speaker or author sought to persuade the audience to agree with him or her. Since most of the biblical text is oratorical, seeking to persuade its audience of some belief or course of action, the study of the rhetorical style in biblical narratives is a natural undertaking.

Rhetorical criticism seeks to expose how the biblical text dramatically affects the audience that hears or reads it. To this end practitioners focus upon literary devices—metaphors, poetic allusions, clever wordplays (especially in the oral form), allusions to other biblical texts (intertextual references), double entendre, humor, strings of rhetorical questions (as in the divine speeches in Job 38–39), and other clever and sophisticated communication tools that biblical authors employed. These were designed to create an impression upon the audience that heard or read the text, and the modern scholar studies how that was accomplished. The early use of the term *aesthetic criticism* emphasized how these scholars sought to appreciate and beauty of the biblical text and affirm it as a work of art. Often advocates of the method refer to Aristotle's *Art of Rhetoric* and say that the method truly begins with him.

If we distinguish between rhetorical and aesthetic criticism, it might be said that rhetorical critics appreciate the literary techniques that provide unity in a passage and also the literary techniques that make a text persuasive to its audience, while aesthetic critics appreciate the literary artistry as a whole. A variation on these methods is structural criticism, which is more directly concerned with the structures within a text that provide unity to the passage and challenge the tendency of historical critics to dissect it.

Often rhetorical and structural critics eschew any attempt to divide a text into sources or subunits, as source critics and traditio-historical critics might; as I've discussed, source critics and traditio-historical critics might see separate literary units as brought together by an editor, or see a piece of literature as having grown and evolved over time. Rhetorical or structuralist critics, whom I'm calling the new literary critics, often enough engage practitioners of the methods we have surveyed in order to maintain the unity of a particular biblical narrative, and to level veiled criticisms of more established critical methodologies. They will refer to the results of these methodologies often in order to refute them. They spend much energy demonstrating the essential unity of a particular text and how presuming this unity is necessary for understanding the full and effective message of the text in its original form. For instance, some essays are devoted completely to demonstrating the unity of a text by responding directly to previous arguments for divisions in the text. (See the example below on Hos 8). New literary critics will show how all the words and literary devices in a particular narrative are necessary for the effective communication that the biblical author sought to accomplish. From my perspective, rhetorical criticism and structuralist criticism appear to offer sophisticated, literary types of form criticism, which then might be said to appreciate the art and beauty of a biblical passage after the form critic has determined the shape and the genre of a particular text. Those I'm calling the new literary critics often refer to a presentation by James Muilenburg (1896–1974) in a Society of Biblical Literature presidential address wherein he called for biblical scholars to "move beyond form criticism" to a literary evaluation and appreciation of the biblical text as the next and more important step after form-critical analysis. His speech appeared in print: James Muilenburg, "Form Criticism and Beyond," *Journal of Biblical Literature* 88 (1969) 1–18.

The word *rhetorical* also betokens the agenda of the rhetorical critic. He or she seeks to observe how a particular text consciously or subconsciously persuades the listeners or readers through the compelling artistry and beauty of the text. Rhetorical critics I have known wax eloquent about the beauty of the text they evaluate. In various passages the text might seek to convince the audience of a particular political position; so a rhetorical critic might point to the Deuteronomistic Historian's use of stories to affirm David and denigrate Saul, or to the general affirmation of Deuteronomic values through the shaping of certain stories. The scholar will find clever and artful allusions in the text—for example wordplay and references to other biblical accounts—that, in a subtle or not-so-subtle way, convince the audience of the theological and political beliefs of the biblical author. In the Psalms the biblical author seeks to evoke emotions from the audience appropriate to the genre of the psalms (praise, lament, thanksgiving, and so forth) in a worship setting. In the prophetic oracles the rhetorical critic will discern the skillful use of language designed by the prophet to communicate the passion of the prophet's message to the audience. In narrative stories the biblical author often uses carefully chosen language to construct the persona of a biblical character and the nature of his or her beliefs. The rhetorical critic delights in affirming the unity of a biblical text and showing how it effectively communicates its message with the artful use of language.

Rhetorical criticism is a type of what I am calling new literary criticism, which is indifferent to the construction of history behind the text, or to the setting from which a biblical text might have come. Rhetorical critics believe that reconstructing history behind a text and tracing the evolution of a text through oral and written stages is too subjective and arbitrary. They point out how every scholar seems to reconstruct the origin and development of a particular text in a different fashion, thus making us suspicious of the method. (I once wrote an essay on Gen 34 about the abduction of Dinah, and I called it "Thirty Four on Thirty Four." I discussed the thirty-four different theories on the traditio-historical development of the text! This is what would make rhetorical critics dubious of the historical critical method in general.) They would say that what we have before us is our present biblical text. Appreciate and assess that; do not engage in a wild chase to reconstruct the origins of the text. It is so often the case that rhetorical critics come to the discipline of biblical studies with a good background in literature (or even a degree in literature), which enables them to view the text as great literature. I have personally known many who have taken this route. Half in jest and half seriously they call us traditio-historical scholars mere pseudohistorians reconstructing a past that probably was never there. Ha ha. For them biblical study is an art not a science. Maybe for us traditio-historical critics biblical study is neither science nor art, but a sport.

Biblical Examples of Rhetorical (Structural and Aesthetic) Criticism

In what follows there will be two examples of rhetorical criticism. The first is an evaluation of Hos 8, a structural analysis, stressing its unity, and the second is an evaluation of the book of Judith, an aesthetic analysis, stressing its artistry.

Hosea 8

The following paragraphs are revised excerpts from a much longer article I published years ago: "Calf, Cult and King: The Unity of Hosea 8:1–13 [sic: 8:1–14] on the Basis of Structural and Thematic Evidence." *Biblische Zeitschrift* 26 (1982) 83–92. At the time I called the kind of analysis guiding discussion structural criticism, a type of rhetoric criticism, which evaluates the literary and aesthetic style of a biblical text in order to maintain that it is a unity and not separate oracles, as other historical-critics might declare.

My translation:

> (1) Raise the trumpet to your mouth as the eagle swoops down upon God's country. For they have broken my covenant and transgressed my law. (2) They cry to me, "My God, we know you . . . we Israel!" (3) Israel hated the good, and now an enemy will pursue him. (4) They make

kings, but not in accord with my will, they make princes, but I do not know them. Their silver and their gold they make into idols for themselves. In so doing, they bring self-destruction. (5) Your calf stinks, Samaria! My anger rages against them! How long will you remain unjustified! (6). Indeed, it is from Israel [not me]; a workman made it, and it is not god. Indeed, the calf of Samaria will become splinters. (7) Verily, "they sow the wind and reap the whirlwind." "[When] there is a grain stalk and there is not a sprout on it, it does not give meal, and if it does, strangers will devour it." (8) Israel is devoured, she is already among the nations, [like] a vessel in which there is no pleasure. (9) Indeed, they go up to Assyria (like) a wild ass going alone; Israel hires lovers. (10) Indeed they have hired lovers among the nations, and now I will gather them [for punishment]. They will writhe under the burden of king and princes for a little while. (11) Verily, Ephraim has multiplied altars for atonement, (but) they have become altars for sinning. (12) Were I to write for him myriads of my instructions, they would still be regarded as alien. (13) Sacrifices of . . ., they sacrificed flesh and they ate it. The Lord delights not in them. Now he will remember their sins and punish their transgression. They will return to Egypt. (14) Israel has forgotten his maker and built temples. Judah has multiplied the walled cities. But I will fire against his cities and it will devour their palaces.

Previously commentators had decided that Hos 8:1–14 is a collection of separate oracles by the prophet Hosea brought together by a skillful editor on the basis of related language and themes (Hos 8:1–3 on the broken covenant, 4–7 against idols, 8–10 against kingship, 11–13 against sacrifice, 14 an attack on the Temple and fortifications.

However, structural and stylistic literary devices may have been used by Hosea to link ideas together in one unified oracle. Use of double entendres, puns, and onomatopoetic wordplay may have been used by the prophet to produce a heavy theological message in one unified oracle.

A notable stylistic feature is the use of the Hebrew particle *ki* to introduce lines of poetry in vv. 6a, 6b, 7a, 9a, 10a, and 11a. Considering the infrequency of this particle in other chapters, it appears to be a distinctive feature of this chapter and it may demonstrate a unified internal structure. Advocates of disunity believe that vv. 4–7, 8–10, and 11–13 are separate oracles, yet the particle is found three times in the first division, twice in the second, and once in the third. It does not seem logical that an editor brought together three oracles with the particle *ki*, seldom used elsewhere by Hosea, and placed the oracles together. Most likely the prophet Hosea crafted a single oracle in which he used this particle that he seldom utilized elsewhere. Nor can we say that *ki* introduces separate oracles, for its presence does not correspond to the divisions proposed by the supporters of disunity.

If we assume that vv. 6–11 are a unity on the basis of this use of the particle, we can observe that the thought of v. 5 is necessary for the thought of v. 6, for both verses speak of the calf. The Hebrew verb for "reject" or "stink" is found in vv. 3 and 5, which implies vv. 3–4 belong to the oracle also. The prophet uses this verb a second time in v. 5 to develop his biting attack on calf worship.

The connection between vv. 3 and 5 is also theological and ironic. In v. 3 Israel rejects the good that comes from God, and in v. 5 God rejects the calf that is willed and worshiped by Israel. This is equitable retribution by God stated with literary irony.

Disunity advocates assume that vv. 11–13 are a distinct oracle. For v. 11 speaks of the multiplication of altars, and v. 13 declares the altars have become loathsome. But if v. 11 is part of the previous oracle, then vv. 12–13 become part of that oracle, too. For the third person reference to altars in v. 11 and v. 13 bring vv. 11–13 together, and the use of *ki* in verse 11 connects it to material that precedes.

Some overall themes can be mentioned that link all of verses 1–13 together.

1. Rejecting the "good" in v. 3 probably refers to the covenant and laws in v. 1. The law is mentioned again in v. 12.

2. The verb "devour" in v. 7 where gain is devoured, foreshadows the use of the verb in v. 8 where the nation is devoured.

3. Assonance is produced by the use of the verb, "multiplies," in v. 1 and the use of the verb, "myriads," in v. 12.

4. Further assonance is found with the use of the verb "hires," in v. 9 followed by a different tense of the same verb in v. 10.

5. The suffix for "my" is used in contrasting fashion. The people say "my law" and "my covenant" in v. 1, but then they cry "my God" for help.

In general, the sequence of thought in this oracle actually parallels the development of thought in the entire book. (That argument in the article is too detailed to list here in this abbreviated summary.)

In conclusion, Hos 8 reflects unity of thought. Verses 1–3 are reinforced by the list of particular sins in the following verses, the sins of king, calf, and cult. The final verses return us to the thought of the first three verses in the chapter. The links between the different parts of the oracle are too tight to have been simply the reason an editor brought together separate oracles in the same chapter. Their relationship is too tight to have simply been the coincidence of editorial relationship. Only v. 14 is an editorial addition. The reference to Judah indicates that. This chapter is an intricate unity that describes how Israel's rebellious deeds have brought upon them destruction. The institutions of king, calf, and cult, which unite society, now are the reason for divine punishment. How ironic!

Judith

The next example of rhetorical, structural, or aesthetic criticism is the book of Judith, which is evaluated by Toni Craven. She engages in a highly sophisticated compositional analysis of this work.

Toni Craven was a highly respected and extensively published scholar in rhetorical criticism and women's studies, who plied her craft for fifty years. She styled herself an aesthetic critic and brought to her practice a sophisticated background (and degree) in literature (as so many rhetorical critics do). One of her finest examples is the book *Artistry and Faith in the Book of Judith*. She observes the literary artistry in the book: the wordplay, the symmetries between different parts of the book, and especially chiasms (Craven). (In her graduate-school days the floor of her living room would be covered with charts showing chiasms in various biblical passages. In excited fashion she would explain them to us.) She initially observes that the book may be broken into two parallel halves that parallel each other: Jdt 1:1—7:32 and Jdt 8:1—16:25. In both halves there is a character (Nebuchadnezzar or Judith) who sends out for others to come and hear a message, the character says he or she has a plan, the plan will be accomplished by their "hand," feasts occur, arrogant actions occur, worship is encouraged, and the enemy is described. In both halves, there are actions which are antithetical, thus creating a contrast between Nebuchadnezzar and Judith. Additional syntactical and linguistic similarities are found in both halves. Then when the two halves of the book are evaluated side by side, it can be seen that each half is arranged in the literary form of a chiasm. So the book is masterfully organized.

Throughout the discussion Craven continues to point out chiasms in the story, as well as clever literary techniques. The frequency of these items indicates that the author of Judith is a sophisticated literary artist.

Craven was also a feminist, so her discussion points out those items and references in the narrative that are meaningful feminist images. Craven finds a significant number of them, which of course, raises the possibility that the author of Judith is a woman, though Craven does not make that an issue in her discussion. Throughout the work, she admits her indebtedness to James Muilenburg. As she observes the literary artistry of the author of Judith, it is worth noting that she has great literary artistry in her own writing.

Narrative Criticism

Narrative criticism is sometimes seen as rhetorical criticism or as a specialized type of rhetorical criticism or as a methodological approach unique in its own way. It seeks to read biblical stories as stories in the same way that rhetorical criticism does, and often it attempts to read biblical stories theologically or ideationally; that is, it seeks to discern what the biblical account is trying to say. It has more advocates in New Testament scholarship than in Old Testament studies.

The methodology does not try to get behind the text or discern its evolution, but rather it wishes to discover the central themes of the narrative and to appreciate the literary devices in the text. It is the final form of the text that is important, and the narrative critic wants to read the text, as it were, for the first time, free from scholarly assumptions, in order to see what the text is saying. Narrative critics wish to see the text in its own "story world." They will bracket out their historical knowledge of the text and simply try to see what the text is saying, and so discover some new about the narrative. (They do not seek to find the particular literary devices that make the story an effective form of communication, as rhetorical critics do; narrative critics simply ask what the text is saying. Thus, narrative criticism is somewhat different from rhetorical criticism, but the two are often very similar.) The rhetorical or narrative critic does not inquire as to what the original author meant, for once the literary text has been created, it is cut loose from its author. A Bible reader approaching a specific passage will bring an intellectual agenda different from that of the original author, so the modern reader will find different messages in the text. The text is free from its author, and such new perceptions of the text are legitimate; there is no "correct" reading.

In narrative criticism, one engages in a "close reading" of the narrative, reading it for the first time, free from outside interpretations. Readers observe the characters in the text and their actions, inquiring as to what motivates them to do what they undertake. They observe the plot and any subtle twists in the plot along with accompanying literary allusions. Language is unstable, and meaning can always change according to a reader's agenda; meanings of texts are fixed in fragile communities of scholars who share with each other their theories of the text's meaning. But if the pool of scholars changes, the meaning of the text also changes (Gunn).

One can point out that reading the biblical text with this agenda is not very different from what a Christian fundamentalist does when he or she reads the Bible in a literal and nonhistorical fashion. In fact, narrative-critical scholars say that they attempt to return to the reading of the biblical stories in a pre-Enlightenment, precritical fashion in order to respect the integrity of the biblical narrative. In a seminal work, *The Eclipse of Biblical Narrative*, Hans Frei (1922–1988) lamented that modern critical scholars lose the respect for the quality of the biblical narrative that people had centuries ago (Frei). Narrative critics try to recover that simple naivete in reading the text in order to discover and appreciate the message of the biblical text. I will quickly add that practitioners of narrative criticism do sometimes refer to modern critical scholarship, and they know enough of it so that they do not fall into some of the horrible misreadings of the Bible perpetrated by modern fundamentalists. Ironically, in order to really do narrative criticism properly, you have to know the modern critical biblical methodologies so that you know what you are rejecting. Or you have to know enough about critical methodologies so that you do not read the Bible as a flat document and say something really stupid about individual stories. Thus, I am a little cynical about how these scholars demand that you must leave behind critical methodologies, because they do not really do that.

When you seek out good narrative-critical pieces of scholarship, you sense that often they are evaluations of extensive portions of the biblical text, usually of an entire biblical book. This is different from rhetorical criticism, which usually focuses upon a limited passage or text. Great narrative critics include Robert Alter (1935–), David Clines (1938–2022), Adele Berlin (1943–), Meir Sternberg (1944–), and Ian Provan (1957–). Provan's study of the book of Deuteronomy is a classic example. Their work is similar to rhetorical-critical evaluations, but focuses more generally upon the narrative as a whole rather than looking for the effective devices that give the biblical passage persuasive power, artistic beauty, and unity. The narrative-critical reader, for example, might admit that a particular text was not originally a unity, but he or she still appreciates the final literary effectiveness of the text.

A Biblical Example of Narrative Criticism

A very good example of narrative criticism is the extensive commentary on 1 Samuel and 2 Samuel by Robert Alter, *The David Story: A Translation with Commentary of 1 and 2 Samuel*. It is noteworthy that Alter provides his own translation in order to focus upon and appreciate the power and the artistic beauty of the text (Alter).

Alter essentially provides a running commentary on the narrative. He does not break down any of the stories into parts, nor does he refer to the well-known divisions of these two books of Samuel. He does not try to get behind the stories. He simply lets the stories speak for themselves and comments upon details in the narrative and the overall plot movement. The biblical figures appear as actors in a great play. He sometimes inquires as to the psychology of the actors in the narratives. He does sometimes bring in historical or archaeological information insofar as it helps explain the plot in the narrative by providing details that we in the modern era would not know.

His commentary is not overburdened with minute details, so that you can observe the direction of the plot. The focus is upon David, and his rise to kingship as well as his failings as king later in life. The books of Samuel take up an existential narrative about David, and Alter facilitates that understanding with his commentary. He attempts to enable his readers to appreciate the full drama of the narrative and especially the unfolding drama of David's life. Thus, we can call Alter's work narrative criticism because he encompasses both books of Samuel in his analysis, and he does not focus in detail upon the literary aspects of any one story. His overall focus on the larger narrative as a great piece of literature differentiates him from the rhetorical, aesthetic, or structural critic, who focuses intently upon the literary phenomena of one text or a shorter piece of literature.

The new literary criticisms add a degree of freshness and vibrancy to the critical study of Old Testament texts. But they are best used when the old critical methodologies are not discarded because the new literary criticisms are perfect complements to the older critical methods.

8

INTELLECTUAL CRITICISMS

WHAT I AM CALLING intellectual criticisms are modes of critical interpretation of the Bible that might be called hermeneutical approaches (I believe so), but their close connection to the new literary criticisms on some points demands that they receive consideration as though they are critical methodologies for interpreting individual texts. Also, these methods appear similar in many ways, but there are slight differences between them, especially in regard to the individual biblical scholars who proclaim themselves advocates of one of these particular methods. A very good collection of essays that use these methods in good representative fashion was edited by Cheryl Exum and David Clines (*The New Literary Criticism and the Hebrew Bible*) (Exum and Clines).

Ideological Criticism

Ideological criticism seems to be a type of narrative criticism, in particular, but it does have its own agenda. This method reads biblical texts and appreciates their literary quality, but it seeks to determine what is the hidden, or not-so-hidden, ideology of the biblical author. Sometimes we need to discern this ideology and counter it or read it out of the text. For example, feminist scholars point out that many biblical texts from the first millennium

BCE have an antiwoman bias because that was the culture of the age, and we need to either read the bias out of those texts or reject those texts. Other scholars point out the imperialistic values of the conquest narratives in Joshua, and we need to reject those texts in our modern age, lest they be used to justify war and violence, as they so often have been used in the past. Some of these critics believe we need to undermine the authority of the biblical text because of its oppressive and antiquated ideas on some issues, such as women, slaves, and war. But if we undercut the authority of the text, what will be the new authority for the believing Jewish and Christian communities? Undermining biblical authority hinders our ability to appeal to some significant biblical texts that condemn the oppression of women, the brutal institution of slavery, and the pursuit of war. Thus, the methodology can undercut its own liberational agenda. Also, some seek to reject biblical authority particularly because of what they see as the Bible's homophobic agenda. To that I quickly respond that from my own personal research, I believe that the seven passages that supposedly condemn same-sex relations actually condemn other things (group rape, cultic prostitution, angel-human sex, the Isis cult, and rape in general). One has to be careful about finding ideas worthy of condemnation in the biblical text, especially if they are not really there. You need the biblical text in order to fight the evils that you think you might find in the biblical text. I have attempted to do this in the past with my interpretation of the biblical text (Gnuse 2014). The most significant ideological criticism over the past two generations in America is feminist criticism, and feminist writers have provided us with some of the most valuable insights for using the biblical text in the struggle for equality.

Ideological criticism also seeks to reject the unconscious and prejudicial values of the modern reader who imposes his values on the text. Most particularly, it is observed that First World scholars overlook the oppressive activities sanctioned by the biblical text that would be observed rather quickly by Third World readers, who sense that colonialism in various forms is justified by First World readers when they consider the biblical text. This would especially pertain to readings that justify the conquest of Canaanites or the destruction of Canaanite culture that appear especially in the book of Joshua but also across the entire Deuteronomistic History. One must read all the texts with a "hermeneutic of suspicion," looking for the justification of oppressive behavior. The "hermeneutic of suspicion" can enable readers to use the biblical text properly in our modern era and not to draw upon passages inappropriately in order to justify oppressive behavior. In the modern era biblical texts have been used to justify killing indigenous Americans, maintaining slavery, subordinating women, and refusing to help poor people. In all instances, these readings were misreadings of the biblical text. Ideological criticism has been motivated precisely by such horrible interpretations of the biblical text. Critical reading is necessary to discern the Bible's meanings accurately.

Of course some modern ideological readings are seen as justifiable by critics advocating them. Liberation theology, for instance, is clearly a modern ideology used to interpret passages in the biblical text. Liberation theologians put forward very political readings that may distort the actual meaning of many biblical passages regardless of liberationists' noble cause of speaking out on behalf of poor and oppressed people in the Third World. Nevertheless, in speaking out on behalf of the poor, this movement is certainly faithful to the overall testimony of the Bible, even if liberationist readings of the exodus event are skewed. In liberation theology, the exodus out of Egypt and the entrance into the land of Canaan are seen as paradigmatic events for the liberation of the poor (even though the brutalization of the Egyptians and the Canaanites has to be overlooked for the exodus and entrance events to be lauded).

In response to ideological-critical approaches in general, it must be noted that individual passages that justify oppressive behavior are mitigated by a wider reading of the biblical text. Though Gen 22 (Abraham and Isaac) may appear to justify human sacrifice, the rest of the biblical text clearly condemns the custom. Though some passages appear to subordinate women, the rest of the biblical text seeks rights and dignity for women far in advance of the values of the ancient world (especially laws in Deuteronomy that seek justice for women, slaves, and foreigners). Canonical criticism can counter the ills perceived in the text by ideological critics.

Dialogism

Critics who accept the assumptions of dialogism often refer to the writings of Mikhail Bakhtin (1895–1975). Following his beliefs they declare that words do not communicate; people do. Meaning is found in or imparted to the biblical text only as people read it and talk to each other about its meaning. Thus, the text does not contain truth; the text confronts me and bestows meaning to me by penetrating my consciousness and pushing my thought to new ideas and new truth. Thus, the message of the text is not really found in the text, but in the subjective relationship between me and the text. This can be called *intersubjectivity*. There is no objectivity in the world or in the biblical text; meaning is found only in the relationship between text and reader. The assumptions of this intellectual trajectory have fed into some of the other critical approaches described below.

Reader-Response Criticism

Similar to dialogism is *reader-response criticism* (or *narrative analysis*, not to be confused with narrative criticism), which posits that what is important is how as reader understands the biblical text. Meaning does not reside in the biblical text but in the reader of the biblical text, who brings theological understandings to the text. (Ideological criticism would seek to critique even these theological understandings.) The meaning of the text is really created when the reader encounters the text; the text inherently has no meaning until a reader exists, either as an individual or as a community. This method rightly acknowledges that there might be a difference between what the original author actually intended and what the audience actually heard. The reader-response critic tries to understand both what the author tried to elicit from the audience as a response to encountering the text, and what the audience might have heard. This method also acknowledges rightly the modern philosophical assumption that once a text has been created, it is out of the hands of its author. Succeeding generations will hear or read a text and find different meanings in it, and their interpretations can be just as valid as the meaning the original author intended. The critic must be honest and acknowledge that how the reader of any age reads a text is the important aspect for consideration by the critic, because ultimately neither the reader nor the critic can ever completely inhabit the mind of the original author. Furthermore, when it comes to the Bible or any other text, different communities of faith in the various parts of the world will read the text and find legitimate meaning in the text for their communities (Fish 167–73). Stanley Fish (1938–) and Wolfgang Iser (1926–2007) are often mentioned as leading proponents in this movement.

Upon approaching the text the reader-response critic looks primarily at the characters. The critic asks what they are like, whether their portrayal is consistent, what they seek or attempt to accomplish, how the characters relate to one another, how the characters relate to the actions they take, and whether the entire narrative comes forth in a coherent fashion. (From the Old Testament the obvious arena for these questions would be the series of stories about Samuel, Saul, and David in 1 and 2 Samuel, which has been the object of rumination by literary critics of all types.)

In the Old Testament we may observe how certain motifs evolved over the years, especially in the oracles of the prophets, which took on new meaning as they were proclaimed anew in later generations. Reader-response criticism attempts to assess a text from the perspective of what might be heard in a text that perhaps we have not noticed before. This critical method asks the scholar to step out beyond cultural conditioning and discover how a text might be read by someone else (such as a Third World reader).

Because textual meaning is derived from the text through readers' personal beliefs, multiple interpretations of a text are possible. There is a plurality of interpretations possible in the reading of a text. I use the word *polyvalency* to describe the capacity of many texts to mean different things to different people. I would point out that biblical texts have endured for centuries so that many people may read them and find different meanings in an individual passage, such as in the Immanuel Oracle in Isa 7. Scholars suspect that the Immanuel image has been associated with the Assyrian army, Hezekiah, Josiah, Zerubbabel, a future coming king, a figure sent from the divine realm (messiah), and Jesus. At each stage the interpretation of the image provided a meaningful message to the audience. This polyvalency is even more possible when two different faith communities, Jewish and Christian, approach the biblical text over the years. A weakness of reader-response criticism is that it does not have guidelines for discerning bad interpretations of a text, which may be harmful, and this permits some of our modern fundamentalist misinterpretations of the Bible to arise. Bad interpretations include nineteenth-century readings of the Bible from US South that justified slavery, or the many biblical misreadings that predicted the end of the world. Literalist misreadings of the book of Revelation and of select Old Testament prophets have inspired people to self-destructive revolution over the past two millennia, and other dangerous behavior.

Biblical Postmodernism or Poststructuralism

This method was inspired by Jean-Francois Lyotard (1924–1998). He criticized the notion of "grand narratives" and not just the possibility of discernible meaning in individual biblical accounts, thus moving beyond ideological criticism and deconstructionism. According to Lyotard, *metanarratives* lay behind biblical texts. For example, the metanarrative in the Pentateuch is the creation of the people Israel by the exodus and the entrance into the land of Palestine. Poststructuralists would challenge the assumptions behind that grand story and demand that we view the narrative from the perspective of the Egyptians and Canaanites who were murdered for the sake of the unfolding of this grand narrative in the biblical text. For postmodernists, this and all metanarratives need to be critiqued as evil.

Such metanarratives also exist in our interpretive agendas, and they, too, must be critiqued. After significant critique, we can move to a freed-up interpretation of a text. One of our unconscious metanarratives begins to affirm the legitimacy of colonialism, especially if we advocate for an image of the "people of God." We in the Western world have taken the image of God's people from the biblical text, wrapped ourselves in it, and justified centuries of European and American colonialism. We have done this often unconsciously but sometimes consciously with our religious and nationalistic rhetoric. Advocates of poststructuralism have generated a host of "postcolonial" readings of biblical narratives from Third World perspectives. We in the West heard their message and realize our unconscious blindness over the years.

Others who observe the movement will say that Mikhail Bakhtin (1895–1975), discussed above, was the first practitioner of the method. He declared that words have many meanings and that none can claim authority, which results in the subjectivity of any reading of the biblical text. All observers declare that this movement is difficult to define because the scholars involved say and do different things. Other intellectuals associated with the movement include Roland Barthes (1915–1980), Jacques Derrida (1930–2004), Michel Foucault (1926–1984), and Julia Kristeva (1941–). Note that many connect Foucault to structuralism and Derrida to deconstructionism, which indicates how blurry the lines are between deconstructionism and these other movements.

Biblical Deconstructionism

A more recent development within poststructuralism is *deconstructionism*, which has as its avowed intention the desire to read the biblical text as literature without any subjective assumptions about form, development, historical background, or underlying structures. If you were a deconstructionist, your goal would be to let the text "speak to you" so that you could hear the message without putting meaning into the text. Then, only secondarily, would you use the tools of structuralism or one of the other new literary criticisms. Even fewer specialists practice this technique. Generally, structuralists and deconstructionists view their methods as a breed set apart from all other critical methodologies; they sometimes consider themselves outside the category of even new literary criticism. Most nonpractitioners, however, view them as sophisticated form critics.

This movement is wedded to the name Jacques Derrida (1930–2004), who advocated *deconstructionism* in the 1960s. He said that words and people impose values and find them in the texts, but there is no absolute truth. We must "deconstruct" the words of a biblical author. According to him, we must eliminate the "authorial construct of meaning" placed into a text by a biblical author. We plumb the meaning of a text in order to discover the author's constructs and then remove them in order to discover the real message of the text. This is similar to ideological criticism, which also has a "hermeneutic of suspicion" when approaching the author's message. But this method goes farther and says we must then move past what the author was trying to tell us in order to embrace the real message of the text.

Language artificially organizes the world, and we must unveil the artificiality of such language. Ideological criticism critiqued the assumptions of the author (and my own), but deconstructionism goes after the very words themselves. We must be particularly alert to language when it is sexist, racist, or classist.

Deconstructionism assumes that a text itself may be inadequate. It may support power structures that need to be dismantled, such as racism, sexism, and colonialism. (Hence, feminist critics and Third World critics use this method.) Deconstructionism also assumes that a text may have gaps, that it may be inadequate, or that it may be missing structures or understandings necessary for coherence. Deconstructionism discovers the incompleteness of the text, which may be fulfilled by the "indeterminacy" of the text. (In other words, the interpreter may supplement the inadequacy of the text with his or her values, especially if the text shows a prejudice that reflects values of the era when it originated.) The deconstructonist critic must "dismantle" these values and replace them with new values or structures. Language reflects the power structures of a society, and these lie inherent in a text, so they must be addressed. Thus, deconstructonists critique the very words of oppression.

Because no values are complete, and because all values change with time, no absolute reading of a text is possible. Even the contemporary critic who seeks to dismantle the old power structures and replace them will produce something which in turn must be critiqued by a later deconstructionist. There is no absolute meaning in texts because there is constant change in history and society. It has been stated that all interpretations of the text are correct, according to this approach to the biblical text, provided that none of them are absolutized by the interpreter. This is "multidimensional exegesis" (Patte 1995: 355–57). No two commentators will approach the same text and come to the same interpretative stance, because objective truth is not to be found in the text, and thus there is suspicion of any consensus among commentators that might arise in the interpretation of texts (Clines 92–93). This promotes the idiosyncrasy of diverse interpretations among the practitioners of deconstruction (Sherwood 163).

Deconstructionists are inspired by the thought of Georg Hegel (1770–831), Friedrich Nietzsche (1844–1900), Martin Heidegger (1899–1976), and more recently Michael Foucault (1926–1984). From these thinkers deconstructionists believe that surface meanings cannot be trusted, for nothing is absolute except the "self" of the reader, who must be faithful to his or her convictions. Theology and religion are distrusted, for they often support the power structures that need to be dismantled, and they falsely believe in a transcendent reality.

These critics are attracted to New Testament texts that relate how Jesus attacked the rich and powerful of his age, thus attacking the power structures of the age. (I note the irony here that deconstructionist readers actually agree with New Testament texts that critique power structures, although deconstructionists themselves often say they seek to attack the text itself.)

Deconstructionists critique the efforts of structuralists (and even poststructuralists, with whom they are often connected), for structuralists engage in a sophisticated analysis of a text's deep psychological structures and movement. Deconstructionists, of course, say that one cannot find meaning in the structures of a text. In fact, they say that one must remove the structures imposed upon a narrative by the author in order to discern the deeper message of a text, for the author has imposed the power structures of the ancient age upon the text. Deconstructionism is a radical form of poststructuralism.

Conclusion

All of these movements are fascinating, and individual scholars who practice them will do a creative analysis of a text. The problem is that the lines between these approaches are blurry, as witnessed by the appeal to certain great thinkers by several of the methodologies. Also, individual writers seem (at least to me) difficult to classify into one of these specific categories. But then biblical scholars are sometimes like artists, and artists are always difficult to classify.

9

CONCLUSION

METHODS OF ANALYZING THE biblical text have as their goal the interpretation of the text in the fullest and richest manner possible. A critical reader of the text seeks to know the background and original message of a specific passage in order to interpret it in a full and meaningful fashion today. Such interpretation provides substance to theology, better insight for ethics, and inspiration for preaching and teaching. Critical methods make the Bible come alive, and when that happens, the church comes alive.

To date, the best methods are those generated in the past two centuries, and some of those have been generated in the past seventy years. Textual, source, form, and traditio-historical criticisms enable the scholar and the theologian to penetrate into the depth of meaning contained within the biblical text. Depending on whether the text is narrative, laws, oracles, proverbs, or psalms, certain methods will be used more than others. But to some degree, the exegete will try to use all of these "higher-critical" methods to find the message of the text for today.

Literary-critical methods help us to appreciate the aesthetic beauty and artistry of the text and subsequently complement the higher-critical methods excellently. I do not buy into the exaggerated statements that these new methods replace the older methods. For although they teach us the great literary quality of the biblical texts, the newer methods do not help us in sermonizing, and by themselves cannot build an introductory course in Old Testament. But they are the necessary complements to the historical-critical approach, which can at times be a little uninspiring and passionless.

The ideological criticisms are brilliant and profound, inspired by some of the greatest minds of the twentieth century. They teach us to discard our assumptions in the most radical fashion and view the text with new eyes. We discard our assumptions not only about the biblical text, but also about ourselves and our ability to understand what we read. Ideological criticisms are a necessary correctives to the higher-critical method and even the literary criticisms at times; they are a complement. But by themselves, they are suicidal for the biblical scholar, theologian, and preacher. These ideological criticisms can rip the Bible out of our hands as an authority for theology, ethics, and belief. Where are we then? It goes without saying that the great minds who inspired these methods were not members of faith communities. Thus, we must be careful not to lose the biblical text as an authority lest we forfeit the reason for doing critical scholarship on biblical texts in the first place. If the Bible loses its authority, we college and seminary professors lose our reason for existence. Then how do we motivate people? How do we use the Bible constructively for theology, ethics, and sermons? Some proponents of ideological criticism seem to forget the potential ramifications of their work and these fundamental questions. These methods serve us best when they teach us to doubt ourselves and our interpretations, but not when they prompt us to think about discarding the biblical text by undercutting its authority, even if its origins from two millennia past underestimate the rights of women and enslaved people. We must never forget that our modern beliefs of human equality and dignity have resulted from the efforts of people inspired by these biblical texts. We interpret these texts in relation to their ancient historical settings; we should not discard them. These methods should teach us to doubt ourselves but not the text.

Hopefully, this short volume has given the you an idea of what these critical methods do and perhaps even an idea of how to use them in your own study of the Bible. To all students, I wish you good luck.

BIBLIOGRAPHY

Alter, Robert. 1999. *The David Story: A Translation with Commentary of 1 and 2 Samuel*. New York: Norton.

Bailey, Lloyd R. 1989. *Noah: The Person and the Story in History and Tradition*. Studies on Personalities of the Old Testament. Columbia: University of South Carolina Press.

Blenkinsopp, Joseph. 1992. *The Pentateuch: An Introduction to the First Five Books of the Bible*. Anchor Bible Reference Library. New York: Doubleday.

Buss, Martin J. 1999. *Biblical Form Criticism in Its Context*. Journal for the Study of the Old Testament Supplement Series 274. Sheffield: Sheffield Academic.

Carr, David. 1993. "The Politics of Textual Subversion: A Diachronic Perspective on the Garden of Eden Story." *Journal of Biblical Literature* 112:577–95.

Chaney, Marvin L. 2017. *Peasants, Prophets, and Political Economy: The Hebrew Bible in Social Perspective*. Eugene, OR: Cascade Books.

Childs, Brevard S. 1970. *Biblical Theology in Crisis*. Philadelphia: Westminster.

———. 1974. *The Book of Exodus*. Old Testament Library. Philadelphia: Westminster.

Clines, David J. A. 1995. *Interested Parties: The Ideology of Writers and Readers of the Hebrew Bible*. Journal for the Study of the Old Testament Supplement Series 205. Sheffield: Sheffield Academic.

Craven, Toni. 1983. *Artistry and Faith in the Book of Judith*. Society of Biblical Literature Dissertation Series 70. Chico, CA: Scholars.

Crenshaw, James L. 1975. "Journey into Oblivion: A Structural Analysis of Gen. 22:1–19." *Soundings: An Interdisciplinary Journal* 58.2: 243–56

Engnell, Ivan. 1969. *A Rigid Scrutiny: Critical Essays on the Old Testament*. Translated and edited by John T. Willis with the collaboration of Helmer Ringgren. Nashville: Vanderbilt University Press.

Esler, Philip F. 2006. *Ancient Israel: The Old Testament in Its Social Context*. Minneapolis: Fortress.

Exum, J. Cheryl, and David J. A. Clines. 1993. *The New Literary Criticism and the Hebrew Bible*. Journal for the Study of the Old Testament Supplement Series 143. Sheffield: JSOT Press.

Bibliography

Fish, Stanley. 1980. *Is There a Text in This Class? The Authority of Interpretive Communities.* Cambridge: Harvard University Press.

Frei, Hans W. 1974. *The Eclipse of Biblical Narrative: A Study in Eighteenth and Nineteenth Century Hermeneutics.* New Haven: Yale University Press.

Gnuse, Robert. 1982. "Calf, Cult, and King: The Unity of Hosea 8:1–13 [*sic*: 8:1–14] on the Basis of Structural and Thematic Evidence." *Biblische Zeitschrift* 26:83–92.

———. 1982. "A Reconsideration of the Form-Critical Structure in 1 Samuel 3: An Ancient Near Eastern Dream Theophany." *Zeitschrift für die alttestamentliche Wissenschaft* 94:379–90.

———. 1984. *The Dream Theophany of Samuel.* Lanham, MD: University Press of America.

———. 1999. "Tradition History." In *Dictionary of Biblical Interpretation,* edited by John H. Hayes, 2:583–88. 2 vols. Nashville: Abingdon.

———. 2014. *Misunderstood Stories: Theological Commentary on Genesis 1–11.* Eugene, OR: Cascade Books.

———. 2024. "Deuteronomic Redaction and the Evolution of the Decalogues in Exodus 20 and Deuteronomy 5." *International Journal of Research in Humanities and Social Studies* 11.2:19–29. https://doi.org/10.32388/715VDN.

Gottwald, Norman K. 1979. *The Tribes of Yahweh: A Sociology of the Religion of Liberated Israel, 1250–1050 B.C.E.* Maryknoll, NY: Orbis. Reprinted with new Preface, Biblical Seminar 66. Sheffield: Sheffield Academic, 1999.

———. 1985. *The Hebrew Bible: A Socio-Literary Introduction.* Philadelphia: Fortress.

———. 2016, 2017, 2018. *Social Justice and the Hebrew Bible.* 3 vols. Center and Library for the Bible and Social Justice Series. Eugene, OR: Cascade Books.

Gunn, David M. 1993. "Narrative Criticism." In *To Each Its Own Meaning: An Introduction to Biblical Criticisms and Their Application,* edited by Steven L. McKenzie and Stephen R. Haynes, 171–95. Louisville: Westminster John Knox. Rev. ed. 1999:201–29.

Habel, Norman C. 1965. "The Form and Significance of the Call Narratives." *Zeitschrift für die alttestamentliche Wissenschaft* 77:297–323.

Jobling, David. 1978. *The Sense of Biblical Narrative: Three Structural Analyses in the Old Testament (1 Samuel 13–31; Numbers 11–12; 1 Kings 17–18).* Journal for the Study of the Old Testament Supplement Series 7. Sheffield: JSOT Press.

———. 1986a. *The Sense of Biblical Narrative: Structural Analyses in the Hebrew Bible I.* 2nd ed. Journal for the Study of the Old Testament Supplement Series 7. Sheffield: JSOT Press.

———. 1986b. *The Sense of Biblical Narrative:Structural Analyses in the Hebrew Bible II.* Journal for the Study of the Old Testament Supplement Series 39. Sheffield: JSOT Press.

Bibliography

Klein, Ralph W. 1974. *Textual Criticism of the Old Testament: From the Septuagint to Qumran.* Guides to Biblical Scholarship: Old Testament Series. Philadelphia: Fortress.

Knight, Douglas A., ed. 1977. *Tradition and Theology in the Old Testament.* Philadelphia: Fortress.

Koch, Klaus. 1969. *The Growth of the Biblical Tradition: The Form-Critical Method.* Translated by S. M. Cupitt. New York: Scribner.

McCarter, P. Kyle, Jr. 1986. *Textual Criticism: Recovering the Text of the Hebrew Bible.* Guides to Biblical Scholarship: Old Testament Series. Philadelphia: Fortress.

Meyers, Carol. 2005. *Households and Holiness: The Religious Culture of Israelite Women.* Facets. Minneapolis: Fortress.

———. 2012. *Rediscovering Eve: Ancient Israelite Women in Context.* New York: Oxford University Press.

Mowinckel, Sigmund. 2002. *The Spirit and the Word: Prophecy and Tradition in Ancient Israel.* Edited by K. C. Hanson. Fortress Classics in Biblical Studies. Minneapolis: Fortress.

Muilenburg, James. 1969. "Form Criticism and Beyond." *Journal of Biblical Literature* 88:1–18.

Nielsen, Eduard. 1968. *The Ten Commandments in New Perspective: A Tradition-historical Approach.* Translated by David J. Bourke. Studies in Biblical Theology 2/7. Naperville, IL: Allenson.

Noth, Martin. 1972. *A History of the Pentateuchal Traditions.* Translated with an introduction by Bernhard W. Anderson. Englewood Cliffs, NJ: Prentice-Hall.

———. 1981. *The Deuteronomistic History.* Translated by J. Doull et al. Journal for the Study of the Old Testament Supplement Series 15. Sheffield: JSOT Press.

Oppenheim, A. Leo. 1956. *The Interpretation of Dreams in the Ancient Near East: With a Translation of an Assyrian Dream Book.* Transactions of the American Philosophical Society, new ser. 46, part 3. Philadelphia: American Philosophical Society.

Patte, Daniel. 1975. *What Is Structural Exegesis?* Guides to Biblical Scholarship: New Testament Series. Philadelphia: Fortress. Reprint, Eugene, OR: Wipf & Stock, 2015.

———. 1995. *The Ethics of Biblical Interpretation: A Reevaluation.* Louisville: Westminster John Knox.

Polzin, Robert. 1977. *Biblical Structuralism: Method and Subjectivity in the Study of Ancient Texts.* Semeia Studies. Philadelphia: Fortress.

———. 1980. *Moses and the Deuteronomist: A Literary Study of the Deuteronomistic History. Part One: Deuteronomy, Joshua, Judges.* New York: Seabury.

———. 1989. *Samuel and the Deuteronomist: A Literary Study of the Deuteronomistic History. Part Two: 1 Samuel.* Indiana Studies in Biblical Literature. Bloomington: Indiana University Press.

Bibliography

———. 1993. *David and the Deuteronomist: A Literary Study of the Deutero-nomistic History. Part Three: 2 Samuel.* Indiana Studies in Biblical Literature. Bloomington: Indiana University Press.

Premnath, D. N. 2003. *Eighth Century Prophets: A Social Analysis.* St. Louis: Chalice.

Rad, Gerhard von. 1966. "The Form-Critical Problem of the Hexateuch." In *The Problem of the Hexateuch and Other Essays,* 1–78. Translated by E. W. Trueman Dicken. Edinburgh: Oliver & Boyd.

Sanders, James A. 1972. *Torah and Canon.* 1st ed. Philadelphia: Fortress.

———. 2005. *Torah and Canon.* 2nd ed. Eugene, OR: Cascade Books,

Sherwood, Yvonne. 1996. *The Prostitute and the Prophet: Hosea's Marriage in Literary Theoretical Perspective.* Journal for the Study of the Old Testament Supplement Series 212. Gender, Culture, Theory 2. Sheffield: Sheffield Academic.

Skinner, John. 1910. *Genesis.* International Critical Commentary. Edinburgh: T. & T. Clark.

Tov, Emanuel. 1992. *Textual Criticism of the Hebrew Bible.* 1st ed. Minneapolis: Fortress.

———. 1997. *The Text-Critical Use of the Septuagint in Biblical Research.* 2nd ed., rev. and enl. Jerusalem Biblical Studies 8. Jerusalem: Simor.

———. 2022. *Textual Criticism of the Hebrew Bible.* Rev. and exp. 4th ed. Minneapolis: Fortress.

Vawter, Bruce. 1977. *On Genesis: A New Reading.* Garden City, NY: Doubleday.

Wenham. Gordon. 1987. *Genesis 1–15.* Word Biblical Commentary 1. Waco, TX: Word.

www.ingramcontent.com/pod-product-compliance
Lightning Source LLC
Chambersburg PA
CBHW020207090426
42734CB00008B/971